What Parents Say
About the OptiKodes System

I just wanted to follow up with our Family OptiKodes consultation on Saturday. Eric, Andrew, and I had such a fun and informative time with you. This is really important work that you are doing. I am looking forward to using the knowledge to further facilitate our understanding of ourselves as a family. I am sure you hear this a lot, but already in one week we have seen so many patterns related to our specific OptiKodes.

—Martha G.

Yvonne and I really benefited from the workshop—great material, and you did a great job of making it understandable and easily applicable. Our kids have already benefited from hearing about it, and all three kids have now taken the instrument. We've had some discussions, and they have been very eager to hear about OptiKodes and how we want to shake things up a bit in our house for the better.

—Alan and Yvonne K., both MBAs, parents of three teenage children

My daughter started to see Kim at the beginning of second grade. Being young for her grade level, with a birthday at the end of September, she had been struggling with reading since she started school. She had extra support at school starting in kindergarten and first grade, but the results we all were looking for were not there. All her teachers over these very critical years had told me they could not figure out how she learned.

Kim introduced us to the OptiKodes System. We were apprehensive with this approach, but were desperate to help our daughter. Kim was able to tap into how our daughter learned immediately. Not only were we elated, but our daughter could not wait to have another session with Kim. At the beginning of second grade, our daughter's reading level of 8 was way below standards. The expense and time commitment paid off with her achieving an advanced level of 30 by the end of second grade. She grew from reading very simple picture books to chapter books all within this year.

Not only did Kim help our daughter, she taught us how to support her in how she learns. Giving us the tools and techniques to use at home put an end to all those homework battles. Our family highly recommends Kim and the OptiKodes approach. Together they are success and you will not regret or be disappointed.
—Leanne M.

My son's kindergarten teacher thought our son might have sensory integration problems. We went through several months of testing and paid over $3000 to learn that my son does not have sensory integration, but in fact is a kinesthetic learner. In other words, he learns best by doing. Traditional school environments are not designed for this type of learner. Before we met Kim, it was a lot like "working" in an environment that speaks another language.

"Prepare the child for the path. Not the path for the child." This is what Kim helps her students and their families do. By the end of first grade my son was bored to tears at his school and reading two grade levels behind. We decided to transfer to a new school, but were very worried about how to get my son up to the same level as his new classmates. The summer before he transferred, my son began working with Kim. He went from reading the "Bob books" to reading proficiently at a mid-third-grade level by the end of summer. By the end of second grade, he was reading at a beginning fifth-grade level. All because of Kim! She has taught us how to learn best in an environment that caters to other learning styles. There is no way my son would have accomplished such academic success without Kim.
—Lisa M.

Kim has been a lifesaver for our family. My seven-year-old daughter has been working with her for over a year now. When we started, she was struggling with reading and growing disinterested in school. We had tried everything, but despite my earnest efforts, I was contributing to her disillusionment with learning! As it turns out, I learn in a very different way and didn't understand how to help my daughter. Kim turned that around—educating all of us on the different ways children learn, how my daughter learns best, techniques to help her, what to do and not to do. Kim transformed my household from a war zone to a peaceful place where homework gets done without fights and going to school in the mornings is something everyone looks forward to.

—Jessica H.

To our dear friend "Teacher Kim,"
Your grace, patience, and vast knowledge of OptiKodes learning has helped save our children's future. For this we are eternally grateful...

—Jen, Mike, Allison, and Brooks K.

During Robert's final IEP during his kindergarten year in May 2012, his teacher recommended that I seek a new pediatrician who would label him as ADD or ADHD. Our pediatrician knew that was not Robert's issue and said it was more learning-related. Last year, during his IEP meeting with his first-grade teacher in late November, she did not even recognize the child reported by his kindergarten teacher in May of that same year. His behavior in no way reflected the child she had in her class after only six weeks, once a week, of Kim's help. Previously, it was very difficult with Robert, as he would lash out when he didn't understand something, and at times, just completely break down. Different family members would attempt to help him with homework, and since we all learned the same way, each of us were

not really showing him anything different than he was already getting from school. We thank God every day, when we pick up Robert and he reports he had a great day at school, for Teacher Kim, and the recommendation from a neighbor to seek her help!
—Lynette B.

We could write an entire book on the techniques and strategies used to get Melissa through school, but the underlying success story is that through Kimberley Blackburn's techniques, Melissa learned to read and write beautifully. During those important developmental years, because we understood how Melissa learned, we were able to tell her teachers her learning profile, and they enthusiastically stepped forward and used the techniques created by Kimberley. The students that followed behind Melissa benefitted. Today Melissa is a freshman in a top-ranked high school in the country and succeeding with As and Bs. Her reading comprehension and written conventions in the California state STAR scores were at the highest end of the range of scores. But most importantly, she loves school, she loves to read, and she is succeeding on her own volition. She has continued to excel in sports, and will add high school basketball to her sports achievements this winter.
—Karen E.

THE OPTIKODES ANSWER

THE BREAKTHROUGH LEARNING PROGRAM FOR STRUGGLING STUDENTS

KIMBERLEY BLACKBURN, MA

OPTIKODES
WALNUT CREEK, CALIFORNIA

OptiKodes, LLC
1997 First Ave
Walnut Creek CA 94597
business@OptiKodes.com

Publisher's Cataloging-in-Publication

    Blackburn, Kimberley.
      The OptiKodes answer : the breakthrough learning
    program for struggling students / Kimberley Blackburn.
      pages cm
      ISBN 978-09914384-0-2
      ISBN 978-09914384-1-9

      1. Instructional systems. 2. Learning, Psychology
    of. 3. Learning disabled children. 4. Learning
    disabled teenagers. 5. Education—United States.
    I. Title.

    LB1028.35.B53 2014   371.3
                QBI14-600012
First Edition

Dedication

This book is dedicated to the following people with all my gratitude:

To my Diamond Approach teachers Hameed Ali, Karen Johnson, Regina Reilly, and Deborah Desmarais— your teaching has enabled my life work to come forth;

To Holly and Amy—I love you to the moon and back;

To John Harper and Ali Albert-Ross—your hearts and dedication have been invaluable;

And:

To nontraditional learners everywhere—you inspire me every day to teach others about how you learn and what ensures your success.

Kimberley Blackburn
February 6, 2014
Walnut Creek, California

CONTENTS

Preface

Before switching careers fourteen years ago and becoming a learning specialist, I was a psychotherapist who had earned a master's degree in clinical psychotherapy and who worked as a child, adolescent, and family specialist. I loved working with families and children of all ages and did that for many years. When my youngest daughter was four years old, she developed a six-month-long, life-threatening illness. I took a sabbatical from working as a therapist to help her fully recover. During her months-long recovery, I began working part-time at my husband's company—a pioneering education company that sold programs and products for nontraditional learners. Until then I had little understanding that many students did not thrive with traditional classroom teaching methods. I naively thought that everyone learned like I did: that reading came naturally, that acing tests simply required routine study, and that hard work always resulted in good grades.

By the time my daughter had fully recovered from her illness, my eyes had been opened. I understood the plight of countless nontraditional schoolchildren and became passionately involved with my husband's company. I took on a key role in revamping their training program, so their core reading methodology could be taught in twelve hours instead of the fifty-six it took when I first arrived. In the process I learned the company's multisensory reading program inside out and eventually began working as a learning specialist with struggling students. In the end, my daughter's illness truly had a silver lining. Had she not fallen ill, I would never have taken the detour that eventually led me to where I am now: introducing a breakthrough learning program that quickly redirects a child towards complete school success and the recovery of their self-esteem.

When children struggle with learning, it always takes a huge toll on their psychological well-being. Many childhood symptoms such as anxiety, depression, temper tantrums, and anger are directly related to a child's underperformance in the classroom. The performance pressure which lies at the heart of our culture filters down to struggling children as early as the second month of kindergarten and leaves them with feelings of worthlessness and frustration. My earlier career as a psychotherapist situated me to spot the devastating psychological effects on struggling students and also to see the impact this has on the whole family system.

Once I got a taste of working on behalf of nontraditional learners and their families, there was no turning back. The icing on the cake was that my older daughter soon began to struggle in first grade. Something just wasn't right—I knew she was bright and capable, yet she seemed to be struggling. More than that, she was showing signs of anxiety that were perplexing. Her tummy was always "hurting"— later I learned this was the code word for anxiety—and she would come home from school sad and dejected. Her teachers adored her, yet slowly but surely her happy-go-lucky personality withered. I felt that school was a big factor in this, but her teachers kept saying she was all right, and that it would just take her a little longer to catch on.

Wisely, her father and I had her tested. Although we learned she had several learning disabilities that were affecting her, they alone did not explain her generalized lack of interest in learning. It seemed that something more than disabilities were in the way. Several more years would pass before I had fully worked out the OptiKodes System, and I would see how right I was. She has a "reading-dormant" Opti-Kode which matches the 40% of all learners who fall behind and stay behind at every grade level if their learning is not turned right-side up again. Had I known then what I know now, I could have helped her with optisensory learning and spared our family the difficulties and worry that we all went through.

None of us can go back—we can only go forward and use what we have learned to help others. My life's purpose is to help as many families as possible escape the overwhelming experience of not knowing why their child is struggling, much less what they can do to help them. I know how hard it is—I have been there!

[1]

There's Nothing Wrong with Your Child

Is Classroom Teaching Missing Your Child?

In schools and classrooms everywhere, countless children fall behind and stay behind, losing more of their confidence and potential every year. If you are a parent of a struggling child, I know your situation: you feel worried every day as you watch your child lose confidence but are unable to help them find answers. You probably also assume your child is one of the only students having difficulty in his or her class.

The truth of the matter is that your child is not alone. 40% of schoolchildren in every grade level are behind and struggling, but many parents are unaware of this. Few things are as stressful for parents as having a child who is struggling in school and not knowing what underlies the problem or what to do. Most parents in this situation know that their child is bright and wants to learn. Nonetheless, all they see is that "something" is in the way for their child, and that it is taking a huge toll on their child's self-esteem. After many years working with struggling learners I have come to know what that "something" is—it is what I refer to as *the misteaching epidemic*.

The misteaching epidemic is the current state of affairs where the many bright, nontraditional learners are not being reached by traditional teaching methods in classrooms everywhere. Teaching methods literally miss the mark with these students, and this ends up leaving countless bright children behind. If your child is behind and struggling for no apparent reason, he or she is likely caught up in this epidemic.

The misteaching I am describing here is a system failure driven by our national education policy, which over-focuses on standardized learning and testing. Well-meaning teachers have their hands tied to state standards, the most recent of which is called Common Core. Now in its second year, many teachers are voicing their dissatisfaction with Common Core, saying that more than ever they feel like robots instead of valued educators entrusted with inspiring their students. Many teachers are describing that they can do little more now than read from scripted lessons, and that there is no room left for engaging instruction that might reach all learners. In addition, budget cuts and larger class sizes are turning classroom teachers into little more than managers, instead of the enthusiastic educators they wanted to be when they entered the profession.

I have been working with struggling, nontraditional students for over fourteen years. I have developed a program which consistently gets these struggling students to grade level and beyond. The program this book introduces—the OptiKodes System—has proven to be life-changing for hundreds of students and their families. It is simple, affordable, and effective. As I often say to parents: the only reason struggling students need high-cost tutors and specialists is that parents don't know what I know. My mission is to change that and empower parents to reach their children using the same program I do.

My message to you right now is this: you can easily learn how to end your child's learning difficulties with the tools and resources that the OptiKodes System puts into your hands. It will show you how to support your child's learning in a way that school has not been able to. The goal of this book and the OptiKodes Academy website is to show you how you can *turn your child's upside down learning right-side up* and keep it that way.

IS OPTIKODES FOR YOU?

Reading *The OptiKodes Answer* is the first step in understanding how to turn your child's life and learning around. The OptiKodes System is not a magic bullet. It's a program which requires consistent parental involvement at home. The good news is that the system doesn't ask that you put more time into what you are doing at home. Instead, it takes the time you are already investing and makes it 100% effective. Implementing the program at home results in:

- learning breakthroughs
- less homework hassles
- improved parent-child relationships
- reduction in time needed for homework
- more motivated students.

Which parents benefit most from the OptiKodes System?

- parents who take an active role in their children's education
- parents who struggled in school and relate to what their children are going through
- parents who know that school isn't "getting" their bright child
- parents who want to turn their worry into effective action.

This learning system has changed our lives and our family. We were at a school that was private and nonacademic. Matthew hadn't been taught to read yet. In order to get him to a better school, he needed to know how to read. We began at the end of May, and he wasn't reading. By September, he was reading at a mid-

dle school level in three months through this system. Not only is he reading, but he's understanding what he's reading. —Lisa M.

COST COMPARISON

When students struggle and classroom teachers cannot get them to grade level, many parents must seek outside help, which usually begins with a diagnostic assessment. This first assessment is a flat fee in the neighborhood of $5000, and the costs go up from there. They include fees for a resource specialist during the school year and often an intensive summer program. It is also not uncommon for some or all of the family to need psychological counseling to deal with the many emotional issues that develop when a child struggles in school. As the chart below shows, one year of conventional support services can cost thousands of dollars.

CONVENTIONAL SUPPORT SERVICES

Diagnostic Testing	$5,000
Family Psychotherapy	$3,600
Resource Specialist	$6,000
Summer Program	$4,000
TOTAL	**$18,600**

By comparison, the OptiKodes Academy program will cost you less than $500 the first year. How can this program be so inexpensive and yet still be effective, you may wonder? The answer is simple: there is nothing wrong with your child. He or she is simply—and tragically—in a traditional school setting that doesn't offer them the student-centric approach they need to thrive. Learning to support your child the way they need at home has a much more powerful effect on your child, and they will be able to take their success into the classroom and thrive.

OPTIKODES

Book	$12
Academy Membership	$179
Consultations	$75–$300
TOTAL	**$266–$491**

You will be seeing the term "optisensory" in the following questionnaire and throughout the book, so I want to define it before you take the questionnaire. *Optisensory learning* is the kind of learning a child does when they learn according to their OptiKode, not according to a standardized approach. The power of optisensory learning lies in the exact fit between a students' OptiKode and the learning strategies that they are matched with. Multisensory methods can still fail to hit the target with a nontraditional learner. Optisensory learning provides the perfect fit for each learner and enables them to finally take off and love the feeling of learning when they use it.

The stress, hassle, and family issues you have been dealing with will begin to dissolve as learning finally starts to land with your child. The simplicity and cost is one of the big mind-blowers for parents who begin using optisensory learning. Once they get that nothing is wrong with their child, and that optisensory learning tools can make such an immediate difference, parents ask, "Why have we just spent all this money on other programs and gotten nowhere? Why don't schools know this?"

It is important to make a distinction between a student who is learning-disabled and all the nontraditional students who are being left behind. The OptiKodes System is designed for the latter group: those learners who do not have other significant learning delays or challenges that require other therapies. The vast majority of the 40% of struggling students who are being left behind by the misteaching epidemic can have a complete turnaround in their abilities when parents take the lead and implement this system at home. At the same time, students with learning disabilities also do better when optisensory learning is added to the other interventions they are receiving.

[2]

The Misteaching Epidemic

WHEN TEACHING MISSES THE MARK

In this book, on the website, in talks, and elsewhere, I say that 40% of schoolchildren struggle and are at risk of falling behind and staying behind with traditional teaching methods. Where do I get this figure? First, let me clarify that I am not saying that 40% of children are failing. I am saying that 40% are behind and struggling, some more than others: *40% are not at grade level in core standards.*

According to a report released in late 2011 by the National Center for Education Statistics, 33% of all students in the fourth grade read below the basic level, and 24% of all eighth-grade students read below the basic level.

The latest National Assessment of Educational Progress from the U.S. Department of Education shows that just 38% of twelfth-graders are proficient in reading, and only 26% are proficient in math.

The annual Diplomas Count report tracks graduation rates across the country and calculated the national average at 74.7% for the class of 2010, the most recent year for which data is available.

According to the National Center for Educational Statistics, 34% of public school students performed at or above "proficient" in reading in 2013 at grades four and eight. This means 66% of students only have basic skills or less.

These national figures clearly indicate that 30% of schoolchildren are struggling and falling behind. This is the same percentage of OptiKodes that are at risk for underperformance in traditional classrooms due to the emphasis on reading-based instruction and learning. (See "The Four Corners of the OptiKodes System" on page 45.)

My experience and that of educators and specialists who share their experience with me is that more than 30% of students are actually struggling in any given classroom. Some students are further behind than others, but somewhere between 35% and 40% of students are behind grade level to some extent. The big picture is that there are other risk factors besides having a nontraditional OptiKode which can result in underperformance—they include having learning disabilities, being young for grade level, and the impact that low socioeconomic status and family difficulties have on a child's learning abilities.

While *The OptiKodes Answer* is mainly directed at unraveling the mystery of why 30% of nontraditional learners struggle and fall behind, it also offers a solution for the 5–10% of other at-risk learners who can be supported with the OptiKodes System to catch up and hold their own in school. Beyond that, the OptiKodes System can offer invaluable support to any traditional learner who is contending with high workloads and homework demands on an ongoing basis.

This measurable loss of learning ability qualifies in my mind as an epidemic because of how widespread it is and how heavy a toll it takes on students and their families. The most devastating thing about the misteaching epidemic is this: once children are caught up in it, they seldom recover. In other words, once children fall behind, they usually stay behind and often lose more ground each school year. Well-meaning teachers use everything they know to help these students catch up, yet these students typically remain behind. Faced with such underperformance on an annual basis, it seems obvious that something is still missing or not hitting the mark with these learners.

Since many parents do not know that there are actually many other children struggling, they often worry in isolation and do not connect with other parents going through the same thing. If parents of struggling students actually knew that in a class of twenty-five children, eight or nine other students were also behind to some degree, the focus would shift more towards the system as the thing that is failing instead of their children. As it is, most parents continue to orient around "there is something wrong with my child." Nothing could be further from the truth—your child's natural learning abilities have more than likely been turned upside down by instruction which is only suitable for the traditional learners who make up 70% of the class.

Is Your Child at Risk?

This would be a good time for you to determine if your child is being left behind by the misteaching epidemic. Answering the following fourteen questions is the first step in stopping the impact of misteaching on your child and turning his or her learning right-side up.

Optisensory Learner Questionnaire

Read each question and enter T (true) or F (false) after the question. Tally your responses.

1. Did your child thrive in preschool but then inexplicably begin to struggle in kindergarten?
2. Has your child gone from being happy and carefree to anxious or frustrated?
3. Has your child's teacher identified him or her as a struggling student or reader?

4. Is your child beginning to dislike or complain about school?

5. Do you feel your child is bright, but the teacher or school isn't "getting" him or her?

6. Is your child a natural-born athlete, a high-energy child, or always on the go?

7. Has your child shown relatively little interest or ability in learning to read compared with other siblings or children you know?

8. Is your child highly inquisitive and always figuring things out?

9. Has your child's teacher suggested that your child might have ADD, ADHD, or a learning disability of some kind, or have you considered this?

10. Has your child had private tutoring or extra help at school but shown little or no improvement?

11. Are you feeling highly worried or overwhelmed with your child's school performance?

12. Is your worry affecting your relationship with your child, your spouse, or your family dynamic?

13. Do you feel like your child is one of the only children struggling in the class?

14. Are you feeling isolated from other parents at school and less willing to share what you and your child are going through?

If you responded T (true) to seven or more questions, it is likely that your child is an optisensory learner being left behind by conventional teaching methods.

If the Optisensory Learner Questionnaire results show that your child is an optisensory learner, this video of parents who were recently in your situation may be very helpful to watch.

🕊 Parents Speak About OptiKodes (video) ➜ optiko.de/w

Check out the OptiKodes Academy online to learn more about how you can get started with the program right away and begin getting your child on track and moving towards success.

Kim has made my life easy. Homework and school for both of my boys was a struggle. She's just made it easier because she's taught me what kind of learners they are, so I can teach and guide them in a way that they can understand. It's just not a fight anymore—they're not frustrated and I'm not frustrated. They are enjoying learning. —Mandy, mother of two optisensory learners

UNDERSTANDING OPTISENSORY LEARNERS

Optisensory learners:

- are often very inquisitive and math-minded
- are often very coordinated and good at sports
- are full of energy and unable to sit for long
- love to talk and verbalize
- are sometimes gifted at singing and musicianship
- prefer to learn by doing or experiencing
- like to dive right in on assignments and projects.

I use the term "optisensory learner" to mean a nontraditional student who does not thrive with standardized teaching methods. 30% of all children are in this category. Optisensory learners don't thrive with a large emphasis on book learning, which is the traditional approach used in schools everywhere. The thing every optisensory learner has in common is that they are reading-dormant in their OptiKode. The key to their success is to offer them instruction which is *not* primarily hinged on "reading to learn." You will read more about this in chapter five, which presents a thorough introduction to OptiKodes. For now it will be helpful to know that the term "optisensory learner" is interchangeable with "nontraditional learner." These are the students whom the OptiKodes System is fundamentally geared to help.

The Hidden Toll

How many children have lost their potential in the misteaching epidemic in the last five decades? The numbers are truly staggering, and in the end point to a sobering fact: as a society we have been accepting a very high student mortality rate, pointing to the student as the problem. The high student mortality rate doesn't actually kill a student, of course, but it is the death of their potential. It completely alters the course of their life and well-being.

Having worked so long with the hidden minority of children who struggle year-in and year-out, I now see that no one individual is to blame and no one person is at fault, especially not teachers. This is a systemic problem within an education system that was created for the world of one hundred years ago, and which is still in its infancy. More is written later in the book about the origins of our education system and why we are long overdue for change.

Questioning the Assumptions

There are a number of assumptions at the core of traditional teaching that are the key factors in the "miss" of the misteaching epidemic. These familiar assumptions about teaching form a bias that they work well for all students, but few people realize how antithetical they are to the learning process of nontraditional learners.

Here are the ten assumptions I see at the core of teaching bias.

- Each child is able to learn best by reading books and by using worksheets and study guides to solidify understanding.
- Each child can easily sit for long periods at a desk and maintain peak focus and efficiency.

- Aside from reading, students only need to learn new information by listening and do not need to discuss it verbally to master it.
- Quiet in the classroom is essential for all students to focus and learn.
- Hands-on and experiential learning is only needed in small doses and mostly with science.
- Children learn best in large groups versus small groups, partners, or one-on-one.
- There is a limited role for doing and movement in learning.
- Standardized tests are an accurate measure of learning and mastery.
- All children should be able to learn in the classroom at a similar pace.
- Whole-language reading methods are as good as or superior to phonics-based instruction. (The "whole language approach" is a method of teaching children to read by recognizing words as whole pieces of language. Proponents of the whole-language philosophy believe that language should not be broken down into letters and combinations of letters and "decoded.")

I am hoping that as you read these assumptions, you see the underlying belief that they serve all students equally well. In my opinion, they really serve a "one size fits all" model of teaching that misses the individual needs of many students. If you are a parent who struggled in school yourself, did reading this list take you back to when you were in the classroom and how the teaching bias disempowered you as a learner? Do you see how it is undermining your child now?

What then is the solution to the negative effects of this bias? Here is a set of "student-centric" guidelines, which if adopted, would end up reaching all the learners in a classroom.

- Each child learns best when his or her learning is synced to their OptiKode.
- Most children lose focus and efficiency when they sit for long periods and leave their body out of learning.
- There are five modalities that all children learn with. Books engage only one modality. The other four modalities should be equally weighted in all classroom instruction.
- Many children need to have audio input to learn well. Options for music and verbal discussion are essential for hearing-dominant learners.
- Hands-on learning throughout the day keeps children engaged in learning. Skillful teachers will find ways to weave experiential learning into all aspects of the curriculum.
- A variety of learning groups is best in the classroom—whole class, small group, partners, and individual learning. Rotating between them and finding the right balance supports students best.
- Students learn best by accessing their moving modality to learn in the classroom, not just during recess, lunch, and PE.
- Standardized tests measure the abilities of traditional learners who have a natural ability to memorize. These tests do not measure interest in learning, artistic ability, musical ability, or athletic ability. They mostly measure how well students take tests.
- Children have different processing speeds and do not learn at the same pace. Speed is not a superior goal to promote in learning. It often creates students who feel rushed and unable to retain what they are learning.
- Whole-language reading instruction has been proven to be inferior to phonics-based programs for optisensory students.

I hope you take away from this section on teaching bias how subjective it is. In other words, it is just a set of assumptions, and a very harmful one at that. The student-centric orientation described above goes hand in hand with optisensory learning and empowers all learners, traditional and nontraditional alike. Because this is true, I encourage parents to question traditional teaching bias and not blindly support it with their child. This can be done with comments to your children like:

- "Even though school may want you to rush, I want you to take your time at home with learning."
- "Enjoying what you learn is the real goal of school."
- "Not every child learns best with a sit, look, and listen approach."
- "Let's explore together how you really learn best."
- "My role is to support you the way you learn, not the way I do or anyone else does."

These kinds of supportive statements will go a long way toward helping your child withstand the impact of teaching bias on their learning and self-esteem.

No Greater Stress for Parents

I assure first time callers that nothing is likely wrong with their child, and that he or she is a natural-born learner whose abilities "have been turned upside down." It is a great relief for an anxious parent to hear that the real problem is an education system which constrains our teachers with uniform, limiting teaching methods. These methods do not sync teaching and learning to every student's OptiKode. I emphasize to parents that this is what has been missing and is the root of their child's difficulty.

Not all children learn best with the "sit, look, and listen" approach, which rests on the "read-to-learn" principle. Instead, many children must engage the other four modalities to thrive: the seeing, hearing, moving, and thinking modalities. These modalities must be engaged in a precise, particular order depending on the child's OptiKode. When this happens, a child is supported exactly as they need, and breakthroughs and success follow. Sadly, many children who come to me have already been given up on. Oftentimes, parents have heard from teachers that their child likely has ADHD, other learning disabilities, or is better suited to attend a school with very learning-delayed students.

A recent experience with a new first-grade student illustrates this common experience. He came to me at the beginning of the year unable to read more than three words. He was being pulled out of his regular classroom for a reading intervention every day for forty-five minutes without any resulting improvement. My assessment revealed there was nothing wrong with him. It was a clear case like so many others that teaching was missing him. Knowing his OptiKode allowed me to match the right tools in the right order so that the lessons and skills would start landing with him. Now, six weeks later, he is almost at grade level, reading short books, and is enthusiastic about reading. Instead of it being a battle to get reading done, he is now the one initiating reading time with his mother. This is not an unusual turnaround for optisensory learning, and points to the fact that children are natural-born learners. When we give them what they need, they simply flourish.

> *I didn't know what to do to help him. School wasn't providing this kind of environment for him. Even in preschool, the teachers shared some concerns, because he was delayed in the alphabet. I was lost on where to go. He wasn't diagnosed with any issues, but starting in first grade, he could only read two words. Kimberley was recommended, and I'm just elated. I am so thankful that he's gaining confidence. It's hard for him in class, but now that he has this understanding of how to read, he's excited to open up a book and excited to go to school. It's only*

been six weeks and he's reading! It's truly amazing! —Lori B., mother of a first grade student

🌀 Video of Lori ➜ optiko.de/w

CHILDREN SELDOM CATCH UP

One question I am frequently asked is if some struggling children ever get to grade level on their own without additional help of some kind. In my experience, this is a rare occurrence. Children who fall behind generally stay behind, and often the gap widens as the years pass. The reason this is so has everything to do with the core message of this book: classroom methods, traditional by nature, only reach about 60% of the learners in the class. The rest don't get the support they need, and their foundation becomes shaky beginning in kindergarten. Every year the gap widens, and these students' motivation and self-esteem suffer in the process. How much a student is affected depends on many factors:

- a student's personality—are they passive or competitive?
- the pressure at home—is dad or mom a "type A" personality?
- the affluence of their family and community
- their parents' patience with homework support
- the family's ability to afford outside help
- good parent-teacher relationships
- whether there are other learning disabilities involved.

Even if every one of the aforementioned issues go in a student's favor, a student who is behind almost always stays behind—the only question is: how far? A struggling student is lucky if his or her parents can remain upbeat and supportive throughout their school years. All things considered, students who are behind usually suffer through thirteen years of unimaginably difficult learning. Many have difficulty finishing high school, and fewer still go on to college.

Substantial research supported by NICHD and OERI shows clearly that with-out systematic, focused, and intensive interventions, however, the majority of children rarely catch up. Unless these children receive the appropriate instruction, over 70 percent of the children entering first grade who are at risk for reading failure will continue to have reading problems into adulthood. On the other hand, the early identification of children at-risk for reading failure coupled with the provision of comprehensive early reading interventions can reduce the percentage of children reading below the basic level in the fourth grade (e.g., 38 percent) to six percent or less.

—*"The Right to Read and the Responsibility to Teach," G. Reid Lyon, PhD*

I recently met Pete, a nontraditional learner, on an out of town trip. He is a classic casualty of the misteaching epidemic. He is one of the extremely lucky ones who had enough love and acceptance in his family to find his way through school and eventually to a rewarding profession. Many others are not so lucky.

Pete is twenty-four years old. He recounts how he hated school and how, by sixth grade, it was hell for him. He is moving-dominant in his OptiKode and suffered with a misdiagnosis of ADHD. It's sad to hear him tell about the effects of being medicated and the frustrations he and his parents had with teachers and the school system. When Pete reached high school, he was aware that he needed to take oral exams, not written ones, but his teacher "did not believe in the science that was coming to light about multisensory learning."

When he graduated from high school, Pete went into the construction trade. "You show me once how to do something, and I've got it," he says. But when he is forced to sit still and learn, it "just doesn't land." Through trial and error and much suffering, Pete figured out how he needed to learn. Recently, he changed professions. He scored a 98 on his real estate exam by using the multisensory learning techniques he developed on his own. Pete's a smart guy, however, he still feels ashamed when he is asked about college and answers, "I didn't go."

Added to the issue of these students lagging behind throughout grade school, research points to what is arguably the worst side effect of the misteaching epidemic, the high school dropout rate: approximately 25% of high school students drop out of school.

It is my assumption—and I must acknowledge it is not proven—that a very high percentage of the students who drop out are optisensory learners—the 40% of students who need a different approach to thrive.

Researchers investigating the high school dropout rate say that students who dropped out reported that school was "too hard" or "too boring." This is exactly what I hear from students who come to me for help—school is always too hard or too boring. When a child sits in a classroom and teaching methods miss them, their interest doesn't ignite. What else can a child do but disengage and zone out, feeling bored at school? I think this would be an excellent research study—looking at the OptiKodes of high school dropouts and seeing if their OptiKodes show the at-risk profile of being "reading-dormant."

THE CRISIS WORSENS

Beyond the dropout rate, one statistic shows that a large percentage of inmates in both adult and juvenile prisons are illiterate:

- 85% of incarcerated juveniles are functionally illiterate.
- 75% of adults in prisons are functionally illiterate.
- 19% of adults in prison are completely illiterate.

Source: Invisible Children

It is not hard to understand how literacy and prison rates are connected. When students have not mastered the basics of reading and writing or have dropped out of high school, their life options become much narrower. For illiterate dropouts, jobs are hard to come by or are low-paying. Such a person's peer group will also likely be people who have not graduated from high school and who are also functionally illiterate. The truth is that falling behind and staying behind in grade school sets many young people up to join subcultures that are out of the mainstream and often dysfunctional.

HIGH SCHOOL DROPOUT STATISTICS (US)

Percent of all dropouts that happen in ninth grade	36%
Percent of US crimes committed by a high school dropout	75%
Percent of US jobs a high school dropout is ineligible for	90%

Source: Education Week, Children Trends Database—April 2013

It's not a stretch to see how many of these students could find themselves drawn to lifestyles which end up becoming a pathway to prison or poverty. With all of these side effects of the misteaching epidemic so life-limiting, I feel compelled to ask the following questions:

- As a culture are we OK with accepting a teaching bias that results in so many high school students dropping out?
- Are we OK with blindly accepting that many of these dropouts end up in prison?
- Do we want to continue accepting such a huge loss of human potential?

If we are sincere in not leaving one more child behind—or in prison—shouldn't we find a way to empower every learner?

THE HUMAN COST OF OVERACHIEVEMENT

In the course of working as a learning specialist for fourteen years, I am seeing a trend in children's symptoms worsening or starting earlier. Children are coming to me more anxious or depressed than ever before. I began working with a fourth-grader earlier this year who was so stressed that she would gnaw at her toes until they bled. She attends a charter school which tries to do things in a more supportive, child-centered way. Nevertheless, this student was feeling enough external pressure that her coping mechanisms were falling apart. Another student this year, a third-grader, had to see a therapist to deal with full-blown panic attacks.

Later in the book I share more about my background and what led me to develop the OptiKodes System, but I want to include here that I have a master's degree in clinical psychotherapy, and that I trained as a child and adolescent specialist. As a result, I have always been attuned to the psychological impact that learning difficulties have on children and their families. I am seeing clinically significant levels of stress in children from every school district I serve.

I believe this is a symptom of our society becoming more and more achievement-oriented. In a nutshell—the heat is on starting day one of kindergarten. Children in kindergarten are now put on a fast track with reading, and the gauntlet is thrown down very early in terms of assessing their reading skills. By December of kindergarten parents get quick feedback if their child is not progressing along with fast-paced state standards. This would have been unthinkable even ten years ago. But those simple days are over. Children in preschool are feeling levels of pressure and stress that would surprise many people.

All this overachievement reminds me of the "frog in the frying pan" experiment. In the experiment, a frog is put in a frying pan filled with tepid water where it sits comfortably at first. The heat is then turned on underneath the pan and the water gradually gets hotter. Amazingly, the frog never jumps out—why is this? The answer has to do with adaptation: the frog keeps adapting to the hotter and hotter water and learns to tolerate it rather than jump out and save himself. As a society, I believe we are in the same predicament with overachievement. We keep adjusting our capacity to tolerate higher and higher levels of stress and keep justifying it as an unavoidable feature of modern life.

This overachievement now starts on day one of kindergarten and arches all the way across the K–12 spectrum. Most parents of high school students are unaware of the long-term consequences of this overachievement pressure and how much homework is burdening their children. Most juniors and seniors are chronically sleep-deprived. They are not getting adequate nutrition or exercise much of the time. All in the name of making the grades and trying to get a 4.5 grade point average to get into the best colleges and universities in the country. Isn't it an irony that we think this standard of overachievement will provide our children with a better quality of life, when in fact it is undermining their well being so profoundly?

Students' anxiety around succeeding has detrimental effects on learning and takes many forms. Diane Pope found that more than 30% of high school students and 15% of middle school students were doing more than three and a half hours of homework per night, but their perception of its usefulness was very low. Only 20–30% of students felt homework was useful.

On top of that homework load, Pope found that 85% of students participate in extracurricular activities that take up a large portion of time. On average, middle school students spent almost seven hours a week on extracurricular activities, and the average high school student spent ten and a half hours. Between school, homework and extracurricular commitments, high school students on average get less than seven hours of sleep per night, when they should be getting nine.

Here are some questions worth considering in light of all this overachievement.

- When did it become no longer good enough to get a 4.0 GPA?
- Who devised this system where getting anything less than straight As all four years of high school would kick a student out of the running to get into the colleges of their choice?

- If we are not okay with all of this, how do we change it?

THERE'S NO TIME TO WASTE

The earlier parents begin using the OptiKodes System, the quicker their child's self-esteem will recover. Students who begin the system by second grade often cannot remember that they ever struggled. On the other hand, students who come in fourth grade or later often have longer-lasting emotional issues. This is because a student's negative self-concept forms right alongside the pain and difficulty they are experiencing in school, resulting in low self-esteem and feelings of worthlessness. Learning difficulties become long-lasting psychological issues if they go unresolved. It makes good sense for parents to act as early as possible and save their child and themselves unnecessary hardship in the long run.

DON'T WAIT FOR YOUR CHILD TO BE LABELED DISABLED

If your child is struggling at school there is a very good chance they will become labeled as learning-disabled. This may have happened already. The hardest thing for me to accept in connection with the misteaching epidemic is the way in which optisensory students are often misunderstood as being disabled, when in fact they simply have an OptiKode which puts them at risk in the traditional classroom.

While many teachers are doing their best to use multisensory techniques in the classroom, without knowing the specifics of a child's learning pattern, their well-intended efforts still miss the mark. Some teachers use more nontraditional methods than others, but I like to explain to open-minded educators that the relatively small fraction they are using is still not enough for the optisensory learner. Such a learner is put at a huge disadvantage in a classroom where the prevailing emphasis remains "read-to-learn." He or she needs reading to be deemphasized. The other modalities you will soon read about need to be brought more front-and-center.

I like to pose this question to participants in an OptiKodes workshop: can you imagine a kind of teaching where reading books and worksheets were the very last things used by a teacher? Many people cannot imagine such a method. As you continue reading, you will come to know firsthand what that kind of teaching—optisensory teaching—would look like. The case studies in chapter six will give you a real feel for the difference between traditional teaching and optisensory teaching. This is what the OptiKodes Academy trains parents to use at home to create learning breakthroughs with their child.

[3]

Each OptiKode: A Specialized Mind

No Two Minds Think Alike

Have you ever wondered why some kids in school were whizzes at math but others were not, why some kids sailed through English but not science? Likely you also noticed that some of your peers were natural-born athletes and others had above-average artistic ability. Think for a moment what your own strengths and weaknesses were in elementary, middle and high school. In what ways are those same strengths and weaknesses still evident in your life? Is it nature or nurture or something else entirely that explains your aptitude across subject areas all these years?

It turns out that each of us is a specialized learner, far more specialized than we have realized or our schools are currently set up to support. This specialization in how each of us learns I refer to as an *OptiKode*. An OptiKode is each person's unique learning platform or operating system. Much like a computer, we each have an operating system that we consistently use as we go through life. Our OptiKode affects not just our learning but all areas of our lives. It turns out there are 360 different OptiKodes, each one a little different from the next. This accounts for all the diversity in how different people think and function in their lives.

Dominant Versus Dormant

The dominant/dormant spectrum is an essential piece of the Opti-Kodes puzzle. It shows that each person's OptiKode is like a set of nested dolls, where the outer modalities act in a dominant way, and the inner ones function in a dormant way. In other words, none of us are dominant across the board in all five modalities. For most of us, three of our modalities come vigorously to the forefront when we learn and function, and the other two take a back seat. In the following section, you will see what happens when two modalities are tied. This occurs in roughly 35% of all people.

This dominant/dormant spectrum applies to everyone and is one of the main discoveries of the OptiKodes System. It reveals that:

- each person functions with most modalities in a dominant way and the rest in a dormant way
- by supporting the dominant modalities in a struggling student's OptiKode, the learner will begin to thrive in their learning
- the OptiKodes System can predict which students will fall behind in school. Those who struggle in reading are reading-dormant in their OptiKode; those who struggle in math are thinking-dormant.

These three discoveries are unique to the OptiKodes System. They set it apart from classic learning style theory, which does not create the hierarchy of intelligences along a dominant/dormant spectrum, nor offer a way to both predict which students are at risk and prevent them from falling behind and struggling. I cannot emphasize how true it is that people have abilities and potential that extend far beyond traditional methods of assessment, and that each OptiKode reveals how to unlock a child's success.

An Example OptiKode

The image below is an example of how I represent an OptiKode. Each OptiKode has three outer, or dominant, modalities and two inner, or dormant, modalities. I use the concentric circles to illustrate how the dormant modalities are buffered by the dominant modalities.

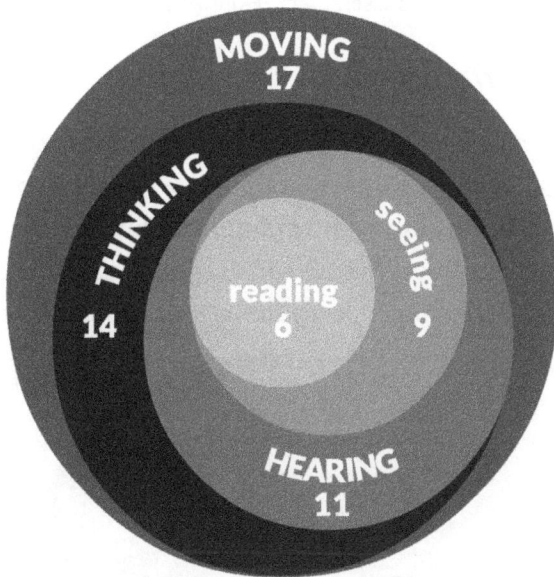

An example OptiKode

The person here is wired (from dominant to dormant) to function as follows: moving, thinking, hearing, seeing, and reading. The numeric values and the meaning of dominant versus dormant are more fully described in chapter three of this book. In an OptiKodes Workshop, families learn the specifics of their struggling child's OptiKode and how to use it to turn their upside down learning right-side up. This understanding has the power to radically change how we approach learning and to get every struggling child oheaded towards success.

Now would be a good time for you to go to the website and get your child's free OptiKode Assessment. The results will confirm whether your child has been struggling due to the traditional teaching bias in his or her school, and will also make reading the coming section on OptiKodes more meaningful for you. The important message for you here is this: there are real answers and solutions to the needless difficulty your child is experiencing at school and at home with learning.

🌐 Children's OptiKodes assessment ➔ optiko.de/3

OptiKodes With Ties

Most people have an OptiKode like the one in the previous section, but about 35% of all people have an OptiKode where two of the modalities are tied. In this example, reading and thinking are tied in the most-dominant position. Seeing and hearing in the second and third positions are also dominant. Only the moving modality is dormant.

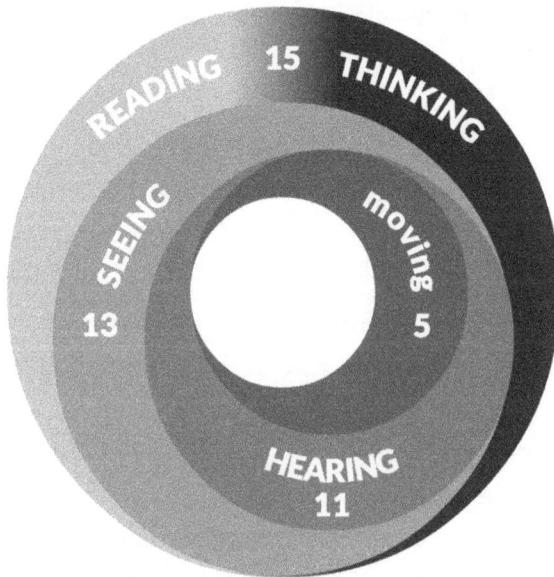

An OptiKode with a tie in the most-dominant position

If the tie is in the first, second, or third position, then this results in having four dominant modalities but only one dormant modality. In a very few cases, the tie is in the fourth position. Then the inner two, tied modalities are both dormant, and the outer three are dominant.

Briefly, ties create both synergistic and polarizing effects. When the tie is synergistic, the two modalities work together and make each stronger as a whole. When the tie is polarizing, one modality overpowers the other and neutralizes its involvement. Being aware of the polarizing effect can minimize its impact.

The full nuances of ties and how to fully integrate that understanding is covered in the OptiKodes training offered through the OptiKodes Academy.

LEARNING HIERARCHY, NOT PERSONALITY

The OptiKodes System is a new learning breakthrough which goes beyond personality. It looks instead at the factors which are more fundamental to success: learning, functioning, and performance. It is a person's OptiKode, not personality, which predicts success in various life situations: school, work or career, relationships, and leisure.

Looking at close to one thousand OptiKodes over the last decade, I have come to understand that a person's OptiKode is the main driver behind their talents and abilities. OptiKodes explain the way we perceive, organize, and function in everyday life. Often I refer to an OptiKode as our "navigational system," because it is what underlies how we function in and out of the classroom. There's really no part of our lives where our OptiKode doesn't operate. I chose to use the root "opti-" in coining the word OptiKode, because "opti-" means "to be the best, the most desirable, or the best something can be," as in the words "optimize" and "optimal." When we learn to function in harmony with our OptiKode, we are at our best.

OptiKodes are not labels, nor are they learning styles. They constitute the personal hierarchy of mental processing that our minds prefer—none is better or worse than any other. Knowing our OptiKode gives us more insight into why some things come naturally to us and others do not.

OptiKodes provide insight into how a particular person's brain perceives, processes, and organizes information. This pattern operates automatically for everyone at an unconscious level. Much like a computer, our brains have an operating system or learning platform that we consistently use as we go through life. This operating system involves the interplay of five distinct learning modalities which we refer to as SHMRT: the seeing, hearing, moving, reading, and thinking modalities.

THE FIVE LEARNING MODALITIES

Seeing "I See"	• natural ability to notice and interpret everything visually • nothing escapes the eye • being good at art and design • seeing things clearly • living life artistically or through heightened visual perception • oriented to key in visually to life • best suited to view to learn • sight smart
Hearing "I Hear	• natural ability to tune into sounds and speech • musical talent • being a good conversationalist and listener • living life by verbalizing and hearing others • oriented to use keen hearing awareness • best suited to hear to learn • sound smart

Moving "I Move"	• natural ability to use hands-on experience • functioning by diving in and letting the body's intelligence be the guide • having good eye-hand coordination and agility • living life by experiencing everything physically • oriented to physically engage with the world • best suited to do to learn • body smart
Reading "I Read"	• natural ability to read and write • understanding and memorizing things that have been read • strong comprehension skills • living life academically through books • oriented to reading and writing • best suited to read to learn • book smart
Thinking "I Think"	• natural ability to analyze and figure things out • detecting patterns • scientific reasoning • good math sense • living life with curiosity about how things work • oriented to numbers and systematic thinking • best suited to analyze to learn • number smart

Once a child's OptiKode is identified, the ranking of the five modalities is diagrammed. One OptiKode might look like this:

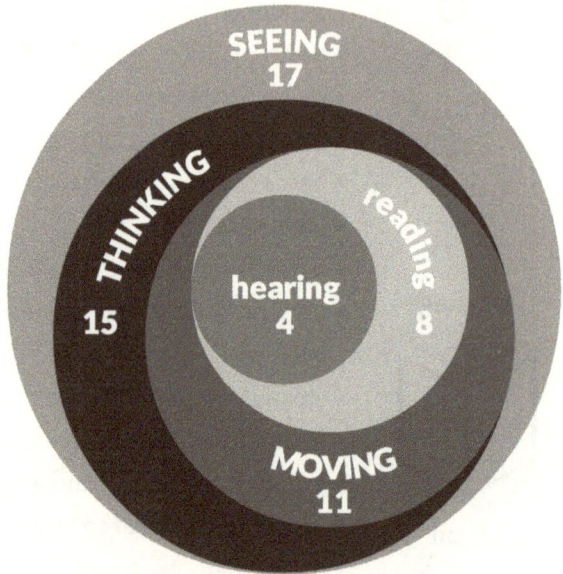

1. Seeing
2. Thinking
3. Moving
4. Reading
5. Hearing

Another OptiKode might look like this:

1. Hearing
2. Moving
3. Thinking
4. Seeing
5. Reading

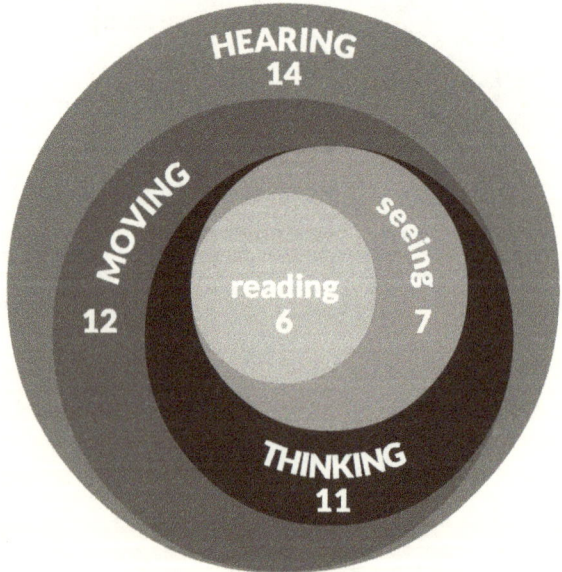

The OptiKode diagram uses the five inwardly-spiraling circles to show:

- the dynamic relationship between the modalities
- the dominant/dormant modalities ranging from the outer to inner circles
- whether a child is at risk: being reading-dormant is a predictor of learning difficulties in a traditional classroom
- how to use the dominant modalities to reach at-risk learners.

The power of the OptiKodes System is that we identify each family member's OptiKode and show parents how to shift out of the default zone of their own OptiKode towards true "child-centric" support. Doing this unlocks a child's natural learning abilities and ends the state of misteaching that goes on for them at school.

Rethinking Intelligence

FROM "READING TO LEARN" TO "LEARNING TO LEARN"

Take a moment to think about how much we learn over the course of our lifetimes. Learning is at the center of our human lives and is involved in every aspect of life. When we are born, we start to learn. When we enter school, our learning takes on a more formal approach and a structure that will remain with us through much of our lives. School prepares us for life and work, and this is a big part of the issue with the current education system. Life has changed and work has changed—dramatically—since our system and principles of education were established.

The capacity for language has been in our DNA for over two million years, but reading and writing is not in our DNA. Reading and writing are a relatively recent development in terms of human evolution. They are something that comes from the outside in—we have to learn them. Reading to learn is central to learning in our world. When we first walk through the school door, we are signing up for reading-to-learn and a process of learning how to learn. Our first lessons are oriented toward learning how to read, language, how the classroom system works, and what is expected of us.

Traditional learners who are reading-dominant in their Opti-Kodes are best suited to "fit in" with this system and how it works. Being reading-dominant in position #1 or #2 of your OptiKode gives you an advantage in most classroom settings—the chemistry lab might be a different story.

Optisensory children need more creative ways of using hearing, touching, and seeing to effectively learn to read, *and* they need to continue to use multimodal learning tools as they progress through school to help the learning land in their short-term and long-term memories. "In one ear and out the other" is a phrase that can often be used to describe an optisensory learner who has not been taught how to use the multimodal tools and techniques needed for learning to land. They could read a lesson perfectly, and as soon as they close the book, they might not have a clue about what they just read.

EXACTLY WHAT IS INTELLIGENCE?

Ask yourself this question: what do you think intelligence is? If you are like most people, you just came up with a response along the lines that intelligence—or IQ—is a capacity that can be measured on a vertical scale with geniuses being at the top and less intelligent people further down. My experience shows me something quite different about intelligence. In my mind, intelligence is not one "raw ability" which can be measured by a standardized IQ test and represented by a number. (Einstein's estimated IQ was around 160).

I understand intelligence instead as a hierarchical set of five different modalities which we all have, but in differing amounts. This explains why someone in school could be really good in math but not excel in reading. The reason being that one of the five modalities, the thinking modality, was probably dominant, but the reading modality was comparatively dormant.

I hope at this point that your own view of intelligence is broadening, and that you see how the OptiKode diagram depicts the actual multimodal nature of intelligence. An OptiKode, in a nutshell, captures exactly which intelligences are dominant and which are dormant. There are 360 different OptiKodes, yet within these, there is further differentiation possible because of the different numeric values each modality may have. All of this speaks to the boundless diversity of human intelligence and why we have such a dynamic evolutionary story in the making.

BEYOND MULTISENSORY TO OPTISENSORY

The word "optisensory" is an evolution of the term "multisensory." In case you are unfamiliar with the term "multisensory," it generally refers to teaching which goes beyond traditional classroom methods and uses other approaches such as "experiential" and "musical." Literally, "multisensory" means the use of multiple senses, not just the one capacity for reading that the brain has.

The OptiKodes System takes multisensory teaching one step further and asserts that no one multisensory technique or method works for all children in the same way. There is a way to get a 100% match between each child and their learning process. Once a child has been assessed and their OptiKode is identified, there is no more second guessing or any randomness left about which tools and strategies should be used to reach them.

Whereas multisensory learning is generalized, optisensory learning is customized and specifically targets a child's known pattern of learning. Going forward, I will be using the term "optisensory" instead of "multisensory," because the students discussed in this book have all been matched with the right tools and strategies and no longer fit in the more general category of multisensory learners.

OptiKodes Benefit All Students

You might be wondering if traditional learners can benefit from OptiKodes. Even traditional learners undergo unnecessary stress due to the reading bias of classroom teaching methods. Even though traditional students are reading-dominant, and can thus keep up with the heavy workloads, their learning is not fully synced up to their OptiKodes either. Traditional learners typically overuse the reading modality at the expense of their other four modalities. This overuse taxes their endurance and lowers the overall enjoyment of learning. In fact, these learners are susceptible to burnout, depression, and at times suicidal thinking, because they are cut out for "book learning," and so they work hard to keep up with advanced placement classes and staggering amounts of homework. All this precocious functioning is a race to nowhere for many high-functioning students. The only place many of them get is exhaustion and demoralization.

These high-achieving, traditional learners can benefit a great deal from knowing their OptiKode and using it to tailor their study periods, so that they too are in alignment with their dominant modalities. A downside of being a traditional, reading-dominant student is the ability they have to easily memorize information on a short-term basis. These students are turning into learners who are good at memorizing information for tests instead of becoming students who can generate creative ideas and synthesize knowledge in new ways.

This is one of my biggest concerns with standardized education—it is not preparing students to think deeply or value original thinking. The school system today is churning out legions of young adults who don't care deeply about what they are learning and who would just as soon forget everything they have just learned and go on to the next sound bite in their education. Do we really want this to be the end goal of our school system?

Some of the most brilliant, creative people I know did not do well at school. Many of them didn't really discover what they could do—and who they really were—until they'd left school and recovered from their education.

—The Element, Ken Robinson, PhD

As an antidote to all this, the OptiKodes System can help gifted and traditional learners sink more deeply into their own authentic learning processes and connect with their unique abilities. When any student, traditional or optisensory, taps into their unique OptiKode, they feel a tailwind that makes learning feel effortless, no matter what subject they are learning. As a result, repetitive, boring lessons have a little more juice, and stale topics get new life breathed into them. The bottom line is that student-centric learning always feels better than standardized learning for any student. It results in a higher ability to truly learn rather than simply memorize and regurgitate facts.

[5]

Introduction to the OptiKodes System

TURNING THE PAGE ON EDUCATION

I have made it my life purpose to unravel the mystery of why so many bright children fall behind in school. The OptiKodes System puts this knowledge into parents' hands and helps end this tragic loss of childhood potential. The OptiKodes System and OptiKodes Academy are part of the new frontier in education reform, which includes well-known sites like Khan Academy and Coursera. Sites like these and ours are bringing cutting-edge innovations in learning directly to students and their families.

Our education system is bogged down by many entrenched forces: government oversight; budget crises at local, state and national levels; over-taxed teachers; over-sized classes; and political agendas, to name a few. Teachers and students are caught in the middle. Entrepreneurs and educational reformers are turning to the Internet to offer parents and students long-needed solutions instead of waiting for the system to undergo the radical transformation needed for today's schoolchildren.

The federal demand that all students will be proficient by 2014 has led states to embrace a very loose definition of proficiency. Most states are now using NAEP's (National Assessment of Educational Progress) "basic" achievement level as their definition of proficiency because NAEP's "proficient" level is far beyond their reach. But many states go even lower than NAEP basic for their definition of proficiency.

—Diane Ravitch, Education Historian

While a more extensive understanding of the OptiKodes System happens in a workshop training, I want to continue introducing the system to you, and then head into some case studies where you will get an even better feel for what is different about optisensory learning. Let's revisit the five modalities now and go more in-depth with each one. They come under the acronym SHMRT: Seeing, Hearing, Moving, Reading, and Thinking.

THE MOVING MODALITY

Let's start with the moving intelligence modality. It may surprise you to hear that the body has a separate and innate kind of intelligence, but it truly does. Any athlete, doctor, musician, gardener, or cook has a high amount of the moving modality in their OptiKode.

The students, often boys, who get in trouble at school for being too active, fidgety, or hyper usually have OptiKodes where their moving modality is ranked first. When they get in trouble, these children are actually being punished for having a moving-dominant Opti-Kode—something they cannot help and which naturally makes them high-energy and less able to sit still. Not surprisingly, moving-dominant children are usually very coordinated and good at sports, but their reading and writing skills often lag behind. This lag is not due to being moving-dominant, but to their being reading-dormant, which will be discussed shortly.

Is it inevitable that these moving-dominant learners will stay distracted in their learning due to their high energy? Not at all! One of the central parts of my program is called BodyPlusLearning. Parents of my students all learn how to implement the program at home. It shows specific techniques to channel the incredible energy these children have, which then helps them with learning. BodyPlusLearning can be used at home as well as in the classroom and is shown in OptiKodes Academy training videos.

BodyPlusLearning is a lifesaver for moving-dominant learners. With it they learn how to do "interval studying" and to keep their body in an active mode while learning. Without this program, moving-dominant learners lose energy and motivation rapidly. With BodyPlusLearning they can stay focused and can manage heavy workloads at home.

THE HEARING MODALITY

Now, let's look at the hearing modality. Singers, public speakers, teachers, communications directors, actors, announcers, and sales people all have hearing-dominant OptiKodes. Like the moving modality, the hearing modality is a separate, standalone ability. People with it often create voices in their heads for characters while they read without being told to do so. They can easily memorize new song lyrics or lines from a movie. There is raw intelligence in this kind of ability. The kids who went into drama and got the lead roles when you were in school were likely hearing-dominant. If you have an iPod with a large music library on it, you likely are as well.

The Seeing Modality

As for the seeing modality, I imagine you are making connections already and understand that artists, designers, surgeons, pilots, and graphic designers are seeing-dominant in their OptiKode. Do you think you are seeing-dominant or dormant? If you often lose your car keys or sunglasses, seldom notice when your spouse changes their hair style or appearance, and often get lost while driving, then you are likely seeing-dormant.

The Thinking Modality

How logical are you and where does that fall in your OptiKode? Were you good at math and always thinking about how things worked when you were a kid? If so, that would likely point to your Opti-Kode being thinking-dominant. Consider your own children now. Do they constantly ask "why?" and seem to have a deep curiosity that is never satisfied? Does he or she notice or make patterns using shapes, numbers, or other things? Do they seem to have a good number sense and like to play with Legos, blocks, and puzzles? If you answered "yes" to most of these questions, then you likely have a thinking-dominant child who will always do well in math and enjoy it too.

The Reading Modality

The fifth modality to consider is reading. Does it come as a surprise to you that reading is an intelligence on its own and that people have an innately different ability for it? People who are reading-dominant in their OptiKodes often seem to teach themselves to read when they are young and typically never struggle

with reading. Any author, grant writer, poet, speech writer, editor, or teacher is likely reading-dominant. What about people who are reading-dormant—what becomes of them since school and most learning is based on a read-to-learn approach? This is where the gauntlet gets thrown down and where so many children are left behind with traditional reading and teaching methods.

In fact, most reading programs are designed in a reading-dominant way. Teachers go to college where reading-dominant instruction is the basis for obtaining their credentials, and they themselves are usually reading-dominant. Classroom instruction is simply not designed to reach the reading-dormant child. 30% of all children are in this predicament. Reading-dormant children almost always have at least one parent who is also reading-dormant. For many of you reading this book, light bulbs may be going on as you make a connection with the reading struggle you had as a child.

The emphasis on reading-dominant instruction in schools is catastrophic for many capable children. Countless students are being set up for unnecessary failure. It must be emphasized that all of this is avoidable and preventable. Optisensory learning at home offsets the damaging effects of classroom methods and levels the field for these children. Later in the book I describe a utopian optisensory classroom—hopefully, it is a vision of the future that is not too far away.

THE FOUR CORNERS OF THE OPTIKODES SYSTEM

As I describe to families in my OptiKodes trainings, the fact that their child is struggling reflects not on their child, but on the emphasis that is put on what I call the "twin pillars" of our education system: reading and math. As a result of this emphasis, all students fall into one of the four corners shown in the following diagram.

READING-DOMINANT thinking-dormant	READING-DOMINANT THINKING-DOMINANT
traditional learners - 25%	*traditional learners - 45%*
reading-dormant thinking-dormant	reading-dormant THINKING-DOMINANT
nontraditional learners (at risk) - 5%	*nontraditional learners (at risk) - 25%*

DOMINANT ↑

Reading

↓ dormant

dormant ⟵ **Thinking / Math** ⟶ DOMINANT

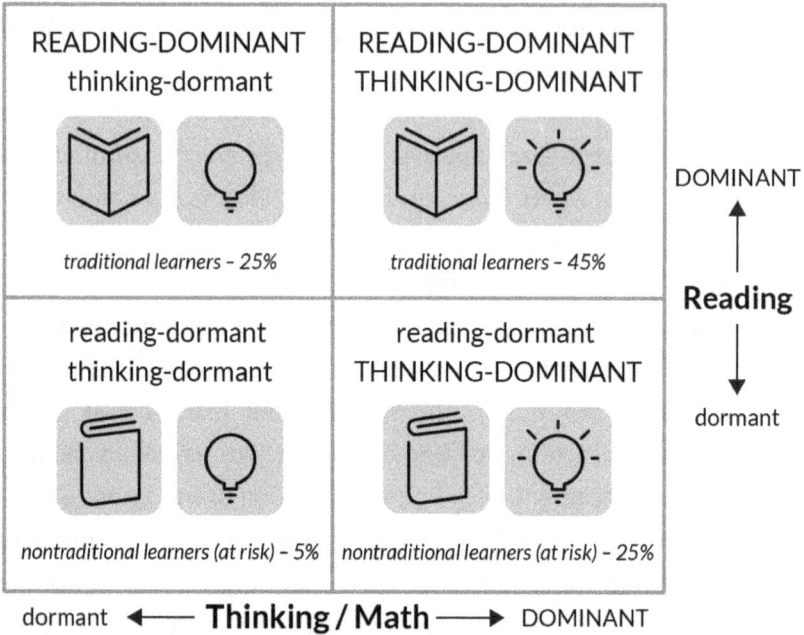

The four corners of the OptiKodes System

Overall the four corners show which OptiKodes will struggle in math, which will struggle in reading, and which will struggle in both. As you will see in the diagram, only 45% of students get a free ride and sail through school in both reading and math.

The two corners on the top are filled with reading-dominant Opti-Kodes. These are the traditional learners who get through school without difficulty. The top-right corner reflects students who are good in both reading and math—45% of all OptiKodes fill these ranks. In the top-left corner are the OptiKodes of students good at reading but not as good in math as a general rule. As I said earlier, students who struggle in math aren't identified and stigmatized like students who are in the bottom two corners, who all struggle with reading.

The students who come to me for help all fall in the bottom two corners. Look closer and see that both groups—30%—are reading-dormant. These are the students, often labeled with having a learning difficulty or disability, who inexplicably struggle each year and whose difficulty teachers find a mystery. At this point I hope you see that there is really no mystery to it: a person's OptiKode determines much about their success. The real surprise is that we don't know and use this understanding to prevent so much unnecessary struggling in our current system.

Continuing with our look at the four corners, the struggling students in the bottom-right corner have problems with reading, but generally are good in math. The students in the bottom-left, however, struggle in both reading and math.

Many of the brightest doctors, scientists, engineers, and innovators have an OptiKode which would fall in the bottom-right corner. These individuals are brilliant when it comes to math and science, but often lag behind in reading and language arts. I suspect Einstein was in this lower-right corner along with other notable inventors and scientists. Which corner do you think you fall in? Did you struggle some in math but not reading? Did you struggle in both subjects? Did you sail through both and never struggle at all?

The fact that there are four corners at all, and that in three of the four corners students struggle in one way or another, says this: school is only set up to serve 45% of students well.

This is a bold statement, yet entirely true. You know if you were in that lucky 45% minority and did not struggle at all. 55% of all other students struggled in math, reading, or both, because we use reading-dominant teaching methods in the first place. Until such time as school-based instruction becomes more student-centric, you can keep your children from falling behind by learning the OptiKodes System and implementing it at home.

LEARNING SHIFTS

Many parents know from firsthand experience how frustrating it can be to try and help their child with schoolwork, only to fall flat and end up feeling ineffective and helpless. A key element in the breakthroughs that students make with the OptiKodes System is what I call *Learning Shifts*. These are the set of consistent support strategies that each parent identifies and uses to keep their child in his or her learning zone. The Learning Shifts are developed using a simple yet powerful formula. They show each parent precisely how to override their own OptiKode's tendencies and to instead use the support that works *according to their child's OptiKode*. Each parent's repeatable formula for success—their Learning Shifts—enable them to finally get it right and to stop the "hit and miss" approach of support that produces homework hassles and fails to reach the child.

This video shows me talking about a family's OptiKodes and will more fully describe how powerful parents' Learning Shifts are in breaking the logjam in their children's learning.

🕭 Learning Shifts (video) ➜ optiko.de/2x

[6]

OptiKodes Case Studies

CASE STUDY: BOY—JACKSON

Jackson began the OptiKodes System in kindergarten, and is now a successful student thriving in third grade. Recently, he was "Mayor for the Day" in his home town in Contra Costa County, California.

Jackson was four months into kindergarten. His mother, Alexandra, learned about OptiKodes at a talk I gave at a local preschool. During the first parent-teacher conference in kindergarten in December, Alexandra was informed by the classroom teacher that Jackson was not meeting benchmark standards for reading. She already knew something was wrong. She suspected in the last year of preschool that something was amiss. He did not learn letter names and sounds like other children and seemed resistant to any part of the early-reading curriculum that was taught.

When his mom got feedback at the kindergarten conference that Jackson was behind, she contacted me. Not yet six, Jackson was already moody, angry, and resistant to going to kindergarten almost from day one. He would pretend to be sick to stay home and said he was "bored"—the code word for many children when their natural learning abilities are being turned upside down.

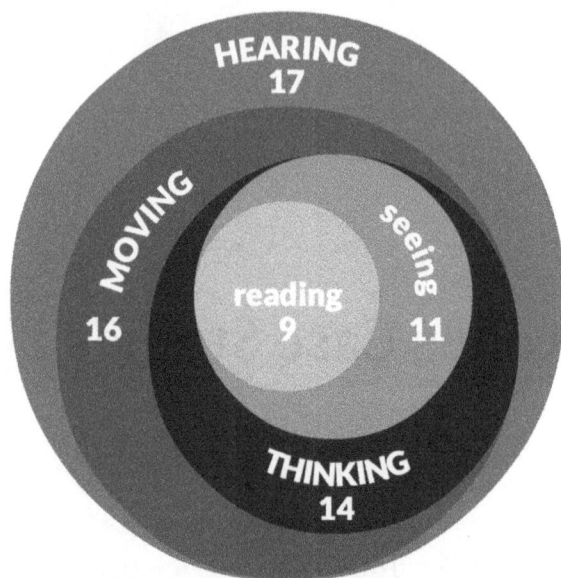

Jackson's OptiKode

In Jackson's OptiKode, reading is in the fifth circle and is most dormant. This accounts for his reading struggle that began early in kindergarten. Because his moving intelligence is #2, he was frustrated because the teaching was missing him. His OptiKode is wired to always do his best. Children with moving-dominant OptiKodes are highly competitive and feel demoralized by "not bringing their winning game" into the classroom. This competitive streak makes sense given the fact that most athletes have moving-dominant OptiKodes. This dominance gives them a fiercely competitive spirit which fuels their training and competitions.

This was true with Jackson—he was resistant to going to kindergarten, where he felt continually defeated by the methods used in his classroom. He was ready to learn and very smart, but a whole-language reading method wasn't reaching him. Given his OptiKode, he needed a physically active, hands-on approach (moving-dominant)

as well as a program that would allow him to verbalize more while learning (hearing-dominant).

Often I am challenged by parents and educators when I say classroom methods are not hearing-dominant. "The teacher talks a lot in the classroom, so that is hearing-dominant," people will point out. While that is true, a teacher doing most of the talking is only half of the hearing/verbal requirement. A hearing-dominant child, like Jackson, needs to do more than listen; he or she needs to verbalize out loud to learn—listening isn't enough. There isn't enough opportunity for this in most classrooms, however. Children are discouraged from discussing what they are learning together. Jackson was getting in trouble constantly for talking in class. His teacher failed to see that without more verbal processing, he was being kept from learning in his most optimal way.

Jackson's third placement is thinking. This requires that teaching instruction be systematic and that new skills be introduced in a coherent, stepwise fashion. Without such a systematic approach, a learner like Jackson simply gets lost and soon disengages from learning. These days, however, reading instruction is often based on the whole-language approach. This approach is essentially an "absorbent" one. It is thought that by seeing language around them and hearing it read, children will internalize the structure of language and become good readers without the need for much explicit instruction. The whole language approach works for the 70% of reading-dominant learners, but not for the rest of the children like Jackson. For all these learners, reading methods must be presented as part of an entire system comprised of logical rules and steps. Not many classrooms incorporate enough of such a method to satisfy their needs.

Case Study: Girl—Jenny

Jenny began the OptiKodes System in second grade, and is now going in to fifth and proficient in all subjects.

Jenny came to me in second grade. Her reading modality is most dormant which makes her an optisensory learner.

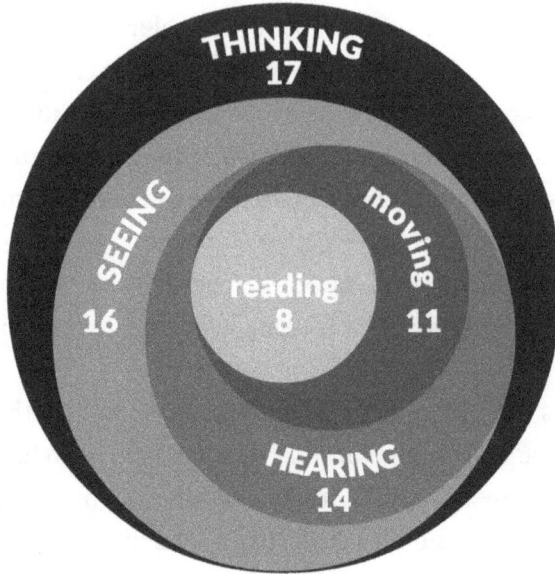

Jenny's OptiKode

Students like Jenny who are thinking most-dominant are rule-oriented and systematic learners. They learn best when they know exactly which steps to take and in which order. Since she is moving-dormant in the fourth circle, she does not have the abundance of energy which Jackson does; thus she can sit for longer periods and focus. She is never disruptive in class but was left behind in reading in kindergarten, because the reading program that was used did not satisfy her need for logical, systematic steps and rules. Thinking is the first learning requirement in her OptiKode and must be synced to her learning to ensure she

thrives. When I taught Jenny new skills, I always presented the lessons in a systematic way which supported her need for a structured thought process.

I always used a lot of visual strategies in my sessions with Jenny, because she is seeing-dominant in her OptiKode. My technique of having her use what I call "Quick Pics" to build strong comprehension skills was very effective as a result. Quick Pics are simple drawings which are similar to story boarding. Students create them while reading. In short, "a picture says a thousand words" is the essence of the Quick Pics strategy. It is also an invaluable tool for working on vocabulary development, which optisensory learners typically need help with. We have a whole series of videos in the OptiKodes Academy which demonstrates the use of Quick Pics in various learning applications.

I want to include more here on what the seeing modality is, because it is often *not* what people think it is. It does not mean using the eyes to read. It means using graphics, pictures, and symbols—everything except text—to aid in reading and learning.

For example, students like Jenny who place high in the seeing modality need to be given time to really look at the pictures in books to glean meaning from what they read. In the early years of reading, teachers and parents of such a student need to match him or her with books full of pictures that will assist them in gaining skills and enjoying the books they read. Books should be selected in terms of the kinds of pictures each student is drawn to, because they are of such enormous support. Making her own pictures, in the form of Quik Pix described above, is even more supportive than seeing someone else's illustrations in books.

A student's active picture-making engages the part of the brain where seeing intelligence is located. Accessing this part of the brain in a robust way is the experience that leads to the development of critical comprehension, writing ability, and vocabulary development in these reading-dormant learners. In other words, this added visual emphasis offsets their reading-dormant disadvantage and levels the playing field for these optisensory students. The key with every student is to use their dominant intelligences to help them compensate for this disadvantage—this is what turns upside down learning right-side up.

Since Jenny's OptiKode is hearing least-dominant, when I worked with her I emphasized verbal explanations and had her verbalize with me as well. She isn't as hearing-dominant as Jackson—he is hearing most-dominant—but she is still dominant in this modality. It needs to take a third position to optimize her learning process. I taught her parents how to do all the same syncing I was doing with her, so they could continue to build on her new foundation at home. Most importantly, they learned how to adjust their own approach—making Learning Shifts—in order to keep Jenny consistently in her learning zone.

I hope you are seeing how the placement of each modality in an OptiKode makes each person a specialized learner. Reverse just two modalities, and you have a person who is wired to function and organize information differently. If Jenny's seeing and thinking modalities were reversed, she would go through life being fundamentally keyed-in visually instead of logically. As a result she might grow up to be an illustrator instead of someone who will likely go into a math- or science-related field. Likewise, if her moving intelligence were more dominant instead of dormant, she would like organized sports more than she does. As it is, her moving intelligence is dormant, so she is not drawn to playing sports. Her mother knows not to push her into athletics, unlike her brother who is moving-dominant and needs to plays sports year round.

Family Patterns Can Be Improved

Variations between parent and child OptiKodes can be the source of much unnecessary tension at home when it comes to homework. Jenny's father, who is highly moving-dominant, often got frustrated with her because he could not understand her low energy or why she didn't have his moving-dominant approach: dive right in and power your way through a project! Like so many parents, until he understood the difference between his OptiKode and his daughter's, he expected her to function just like him. There is more understanding and harmony between them now. Jenny is now a happy fifth-grader who has discovered that she is a talented writer and student. She is thriving in all subject areas.

Four Different Family Types

When a child struggles with learning, the whole family struggles along with them. How this plays out depends on the overall family dynamic. You might imagine an optisensory father, who struggled himself as a child, would be more understanding and supportive with his optisensory child. Sometimes the reverse is true. Often an optisensory father whose learning struggles were treated harshly approaches his child in the same way.

As a way of dealing with the different tension patterns that show up in family dynamics, the OptiKodes System shows that each family can be categorized into one of four different family types, each one being defined by how many optisensory children or parents exist in the family.

An Asteroid Family, for example, is a family where there are no optisensory children or parents—everyone is a traditional learner and no one struggles with school or learning. As you might guess, I get very few of these families, but I do give a workshop for the Asteroid Family, because children in Asteroid families undergo the highest levels of stress compared to the other family types. This is because OptiKodes of learners in an Asteroid family are cut out to excel in school, so children in this type of family can and do rise to the challenge and take on the biggest work loads of all. As a result, these children are most susceptible to burnout and stress. Parents in Asteroid families can benefit by learning how to minimize putting additional stress on their children; these parents need to learn how to actually help their children be "normal" kids and how to not get too caught up in making the grades.

In the Nebula Family constellation there is one parent-child dyad that is traditional and one parent-child dyad that is optisensory. There are predictable family patterns that exist within the Nebula Family dynamic—the two dyads can be isolated from one another, and a healthy four-way dynamic can fail to develop. The other two family types—the Supernova and Quasar Family—also have unique patterns which are investigated and worked with in an OptiKodes Training.

HOME IS GROUND ZERO

I hope by now you see that you don't have to send your child to a different school, make radical changes in your child's life, or spend thousands of dollars on tutors to bring a true Learning Shift and lasting success to your child.

The OptiKodes System is not rocket science, but it will give you an entirely different frame of reference for understanding your child and reaching them in a way traditional teaching cannot. In my opening remarks with a parent who is calling for the first time, I always say, "If you wait for the school to get it right with your student, you will be waiting in vain. Parent involvement at home is the one real hope you have."

If your child is struggling, it is almost certain that he or she needs an ongoing optisensory approach to thrive. Your child needs that approach every day in their lives—without it they will continue to falter and fall behind. This is why tutoring and specialist help is susceptible to what I call the "rebound effect." When your child stops going to the specialist and is once again in the classroom with methods that don't reach them, he or she will eventually lose ground and fall behind again. Then you are faced with more high-rate tutoring and left wondering how long it will last this time. There is another way.

By learning the OptiKodes System and how to make the right Learning Shifts, you ensure your child will be able to consistently stay in their learning zone at home. This is the amazing thing I've seen time and again: it is enough for children to have optisensory learning at home. When optisensory techniques are available at home, their breakthroughs follow them into the classroom and their psychological issues quickly fall away.

[7]

The OptiKodes Story

As a learning specialist, I know one thing above all else: there are as many types of learners as there are children. When a new student comes into my office, I don't start by focusing on what skills the child lacks. I start first and foremost by understanding exactly how this new student learns. Once I know that, I begin matching that child with the right tools and strategies that will put them and keep them in their learning zone.

This is the expertise I have developed over the last fourteen years—seeing exactly how the child in front of me is wired to learn. Each child has a unique brilliance waiting to come forward. Sadly, all this brilliance is not tapped into with the standardized teaching methods which are still being used in classrooms and homes every day. This brilliance lays dormant and is gradually lost bit by bit over time.

My practice is filled exclusively with these nontraditional, optisensory learners. My job with each child is to identify and tap into their OptiKode so that their natural brilliance will finally be engaged. When it does, it spills out like a symphony that is being played and heard for the first time. At last, the student experiences a natural resonance in their brain's intrinsic way of processing and organizing information. When this resonance occurs, misteaching ends for the child, and they finally feel the support of optisensory learning, which quickly puts them on a new road to success.

DISCOVERING OPTIKODES

I am often asked by parents during our first family meeting how I discovered OptiKodes. Parents become very inspired in our first session as they come to see how simple and effective the program will be for their struggling child.

In the early years I worked rather "intuitively" with struggling students. In other words, I hadn't developed the OptiKode Assessments and was relying on my gut instincts. I used a multisensory program with every student, but over time I began to see that I was using different parts of it with different students. They all got to grade level at school in a short period of time, but I was finding that if I made certain adjustments with a student, he or she would progress more quickly and enjoy the process more. I was awed to see how simple adjustments could produce such dramatic results.

As exciting as it was that all the students coming to me were becoming successful learners, a larger question arose for me: what is it about these students that put them at risk for reading difficulty in a traditional classroom in the first place? What do all these students have in common?

Soon it became apparent that each student was using different pieces of the multisensory program differently. Some students were responding quickly to the more thinking elements of the program, while others were literally thriving when presented with the moving or seeing elements. Still other students were able to cement new skills when given the chance to learn in a hearing dominant way.

As time passed and I examined more closely how each student was learning, it became apparent that each learner wasn't using just one or even two learning pathways but three or four pathways. Once I saw this in operation, I began to talk about each student's "dominant three" intelligences and to lesson-plan accordingly. I found that teaching to each student's dominant three intelligences sped up their learning process, and equally important, this type of teaching made it seem effortless and even enjoyable for them.

Based on these insights, I designed evaluations that I began using to assess each new student's learning profile. Although learning style theorists believe there are eight modes of intelligence, I found that it was sufficient to use a core set of five: Reading, Hearing, Thinking, Moving, and Seeing. I found that working with these five core modalities were most critical in understanding how each student's brain approaches the learning process and whether or not they were successful at school.

Still seeking to answer the question as to what put these struggling students at risk compared to those who excelled, I zeroed in on one element in their learning profile and noticed the following: *each struggling student's reading intelligence was dormant rather than dominant in their learning profile!*

This was a major breakthrough, and perhaps the biggest discovery made working with these struggling children through the years. For years, educators and learning specialists far and wide have been trying to understand why 30–40% of children in every grade level fall behind in reading alone. Many culprits have been considered, but the root cause I saw lay not in problems at home, with learning disabilities, or ADHD, but rather in the way different brains prefer to learn! The fact of the matter is that different styles of learning are only a problem if there is only one accepted standard for teaching in classrooms.

As I shared my breakthrough with others, I continued to validate my evaluations and findings and began calling a student's learning profile an OptiKode. As the number of evaluations I did increased, I saw what a large number of variations existed, each one with its own integrity and inner intelligence. When I counted the combinations, I saw that 360 variations were possible. In essence, I see that any given OptiKode is really a snapshot of how a learner navigates. With it, their learning patterns and predispositions stand out and I can predict what each learner needs to thrive.

At this point I was well beyond looking at students who struggled only in reading and started looking at math aptitude. I saw that the predictor of math success or difficulty for a student was another one of the five learning styles—the thinking modality. Just as a dormant reading modality predicted reading difficulty, I realized that a dormant thinking modality would predict problems with math!

Suddenly, I saw the next obvious evolution in the OptiKodes System: it could predict with accuracy who would struggle with math or reading or both. From there I itemized all 360 OptiKodes, and realized that 30% of all students struggle with reading, and 5% struggle with both reading and math (see page 45).

In the last several years I have become increasingly focused on parent education. During this time I had been seeing that parent involvement at home was moving my students more quickly to grade level and keeping them on solid ground there. It dawned on me that I had to find a way to put the tools and resources of the program into parents' hands, so that more children could get on track and stay on track. The thought of families everywhere knowing and using the OptiKodes System as a matter of course is a thrilling one for me. It means that a day might actually arrive when not one single child is ever left behind again. This thought inspires me every day to continue building the OptiKodes Academy as the place to teach families how to provide optisensory learning to their children as a matter of course.

[8]

The Role of Fun in Learning

As a learning specialist who works with many students with low self-esteem, I have a "magic bullet" to deal with their resistance: *fun!* Bringing fun into the learning experience with these nontraditional students is as critical an ingredient as the skills that I teach and the overall program I use. I know how essential fun is in reaching these learners, and every day I find more ways to infuse my work with lightheartedness and fun.

Simple observation shows that children love learning, and that learning and play are inseparable in early child development—at least until they get into school and learning becomes work. What I notice 100% of the time is that fun is absolutely the best support for learning.

When I first meet a new student, I always ask them what they think my rules are. Usually they respond with things like: "no talking," "don't move too much," and "no throwing things." My only rule, I tell them, is *I have to have fun.*

It is always great to see the expressions on their faces when I tell them my one rule is I have to have fun—their expressions go from disbelief to delight. I then explain to them that if I am having fun, then that means that they are staying engaged with learning and, most importantly, they will be having fun too. They get the picture very quickly—learning is going to be different here—and this launches us on a course of a fun and life-changing learning experience together.

The moment students first walk into my office they realize "they are not in Kansas anymore." My office is decked out in pirate regalia—there are pirate flags adorning the ceiling and walls, treasure maps drape the room, and a corner is filled with several treasure chests that are reminiscent of *The Pirates of the Caribbean*. The moment children walk in their eyes light up—they have never seen an office like this before, and many of them have gone to more than one other specialist before me. Right away they get the message I want them to get: this will not feel like learning has ever felt before. Here imagination is invited in, and fun and creativity will rule the day!

My orientation with enjoyment and fun comes from my background as a psychotherapist. That training and experience has given me a keen sensitivity to the psychological problems that struggling learners and their families carry. Every child that comes to me is carrying an unbelievably heavy load of despair and hopelessness. Because of the added performance anxiety that exists in schools, every student I work with already feels quite deficient and resistant to learning and school.

Knowing this, my goal is to quickly help them relax and find the courage to try learning with this complete stranger in front of them. What better way to help them open up, than to present them with a cool and imaginative pirate den that doesn't have a single desk or chair in it. Siblings and parents often look envious when a child of theirs is first dropped off—brothers, sisters, and even parents look like they want a piece of the fun and excitement too.

My one rule pops a student's resistance like a balloon. Think of the last time you were feeling frustrated or stressful and someone told you a joke, or you turned on Comedy Central and started laughing. It is almost impossible to stay negative and stressed out when fun is in the mix. The products I have developed are all designed to carry on this playful and fun approach while students learn core academic skills. The idea that learning has to be serious business needs to be reconsidered so that our teaching practices can engage students' curiosity and their willing minds. The truth is that fun and lightheartedness create an open receptivity, which is needed to ignite the hope and willingness of children who have struggled for so long.

The last thing I want to share on the topic of having fun is how essential it is that parents adopt this same fun-filled spirit at home. I am sure you can see how my fun formula is diluted if a student comes to my office and has a fun and inspiring lesson, but then goes home to parents who think that learning has to be done in a serious manner. It is not easy sometimes for parent's "serious balloon" to pop. Eventually, though, all the parents in my practice learn how to bring fun into learning at home, but for some it is not an easy thing. We are creatures of habit and very few of us had fun modeled at school or home when we were growing up.

If your child is struggling, it is vitally important for you to realize that your stress and worry may be affecting your child's well-being and worsening their situation at school. As anxious as you are, your child is feeling an even greater sense of despair and stress, and he or she needs your calm and equanimity to offset their own troublesome feelings. Parents can forget that children are 100% absorbent, far more sensitive, in fact, than we are. Children pick up everything in their midst. If possible, take a deep breath and hear me: there are answers for your child's school situation with the OptiKodes System, but the first step you must take is to learn to let go of some of your worry. Do what you can to talk to other people—not your child—to express your concern. Here are further suggestions on how to handle your worry:

- Minimize asking your child what they did at school with a tone of concern or worry in your voice.
- Try to offer them reassuring statements such as:
  - "It is because of how things are taught at school, not your ability, that learning is hard."
  - "Many teachers do not have the right tools to reach all their students easily."
  - "You are not alone—there are other students in the class who are struggling unnecessarily."
  - "All children learn differently, and I am going to learn how you learn best."

These normalizing statements put children's troubled hearts at ease, and they begin to feel that the person closest to them, their parent, understands their predicament and is on their team.

Beyond these things, consider taking your child to the park, grab the swing next to them, and swing along with them in the silliest and most spontaneous way possible. Have some fun together and notice how exhilarating and liberating that feels. Find ways to recreate that feeling with your child again and again every day. Doing so will help relieve the worry that is gripping your child's tender heart. You might become just as addicted to fun as I have in the process.

🌐 The role of fun in learning (video) → optiko.de/3j

[9]

My OptiKode

Thinking back to the four corners of the OptiKodes System (page 45), I wanted to share that I am a member of the upper-right group where both reading and thinking modalities are dominant. As is true with everyone in that corner, it was simply the luck of the draw that got me into that corner. Simply put, my mother is dominant in both reading and thinking modalities, and by chance I took after her.

My father, on the other hand, places in the lower-right corner, because he is reading-dormant and thinking-dominant. Of the three children my parents had, two of us have OptiKodes like my mother's, and one of us has my father's OptiKode. This is a very common thing. When there is one optisensory parent and one traditional parent, there is usually one of each among their children. The thing to emphasize here is that your OptiKode is completely random—no one gets to pick their OptiKode. As it was, both my brother and I who are reading- and thinking-dominant went on to college; my nontraditional, optisensory brother did not. This is often the case with optisensory learners—school and

learning is typically too hard and frustrating to continue, the likes of which traditional learners cannot even imagine. As a result, optisensory learners often do not go on to college. Sadly, my brother has always thought he is not as smart as his two older siblings. Nothing could be further from the truth.

When I meet optisensory learners who went to college and made it through, I am deeply impressed. In fact, I am far more impressed with them than with my own ability to earn two college degrees. An optisensory learner who completes an undergraduate degree has climbed an unbelievably high mountain and worked ten times harder than someone like me to get through. I honestly don't know how any optisensory learner finds the motivation and perseverance to get through college after thirteen years of school that have already been so tough.

LEVELING THE PLAYING FIELD AT HOME

One of the endlessly amazing things for me about how OptiKodes changes students' lives is how quickly it does its magic and how little time investment is needed for the program to create breakthroughs. How can it be, I still ask myself, that a child can attend school thirty hours a week, sometimes for years on end, without experiencing success, and then so rapidly mobilize skills and success with the OptiKodes System? Furthermore, how can a child experience optisensory learning for just an hour or two with me each week for a period of months, and then have that be enough for them to go into the classroom every day and be able to contend with the traditional bias that once set them back?

The answer to that question is this: human beings in general, and especially children, are extremely resilient. When it comes to learning, if children are presented with even a little bit of what they need, they catch fire and take off. When this happens, a new day has dawned for them. They can and do go into their classrooms and thrive, even when nothing has changed in the classroom.

A parallel example of resiliency has to do with children who have been traumatized in some way during childhood. The children who overcome extreme situations in childhood and go on to become healthy adults all have one thing in common: there was at least one person in their life who demonstrated a measure of love and support for them. Even a small but meaningful amount of support some-where in these children's difficult lives offsets some of the effects of their neglect or abuse.

The same thing seems to go on when it comes to the ability to learn well. If a child is marooned unendingly in the classroom with methods that don't reach them, they are usually derailed and unin-tentionally left behind. On the other hand, just a few hours a week of the right student-centric teaching methods is all that is needed for these learners to engage their inner resources and make an almost miraculous recovery of their natural learning abilities. I do think this is part of the answer to the mystery of how so little can go such a long way for these learners. Every child is a natural-born learner, and only a little engagement of their natural abilities is needed to break the logjam. This should come as a very hopeful fact for parents and open-minded educators.

If teachers truly knew the small amount of student-centric teach-ing that is needed to reach the optisensory learners in their classes, I believe they would be eager to learn how to assess the OptiKodes of their students and begin to reach them with the tools and techniques they need so badly. My message is that it doesn't require revamping a teacher's entire curriculum to engage each optisensory student. As students learn new tools and techniques at home, a teacher's willing-ness to embrace some of how they learn best in the classroom will build on the success that has started at home. The good news is that optisensory teaching is contagious. It liberates minds, hearts, and abilities as students and teachers experience this fresh, multimodal way of learning.

The OptiKodes System does not require perfection. Children are resilient, and they will take anything you offer them and run with it. Thirty minutes or more a day at home coaching your child to use the Learning Shifts will create a powerful awakening in them. These Learning Shifts will finally bring your child an effortless and successful learning experience, and it is this breakthrough that will help them see that they are smart and capable. The lasting attitude change that follows is the real transformation that children stand on when they go into class each day.

This is why I like to say that home is "ground zero" for OptiKodes and that parents have the power to level the playing field for their children who have been unintentionally handicapped. In a day and age when budget cuts of all kinds are impacting schools, the good news is that home is the new frontier where each family can do its part to supplement their child's education. As we all know, parents are already committing many hours every week in homework help and are often finding periodic tutors to supplement their children's learning as well.

Optisensory learning is in line with this greater movement towards parents doing their growing part at home. Every parent basically wants to be as effective as they can be can be with their children. Again, my whole premise is that for most struggling students, their learning is not the problem. Even those students who have disabilities are often being handicapped by something far different than the things they are diagnosed with: teaching methods that are mismatched with the way their brains prefer to process information.

Time and again, I have had students start with me who have learning disabilities and who have had treatment for those disorders by other specialists. Despite these interventions, they are still behind when their desperate parents find me. The thing that was not uncovered was how their child learned best. Ultimately, tutors, specialists, and special education teachers were still teaching them in the same mismatched way.

How Long Children Need My Support

It is always hard to pinpoint for parents exactly how long it will take for their child to get to grade level using the OptiKodes System. It depends on several factors.

- How far behind is a student when they first start coming?
- What is their OptiKode configuration? Some codes go a little faster than others. Generally, students who are very thinking- and moving-dominant move a little faster, although all of my students move through more quickly than with other conventional tutoring programs. This is because most conventional tutoring programs, like school-based intervention programs, don't offer anything truly different than the traditional curriculum already used in the classroom. The only real difference is that they are getting intervention on a one-on-one basis rather than in a whole-group environment.
- How much psychological stress has a child's difficulty caused in them, and how much resistance to learning has developed? As I described earlier, the more moving-dominant children are, the more overwhelmed and frustrated they usually become. Kids who are very oppositional and defiant take longer to respond, but eventually, they too come around when their trust builds and when they see how optisensory tools are helping them.
- Does a parent integrate optisensory learning fully at home? The more a family mirrors what I do at home, the faster their child will get to grade level and stay there.

When all is said and done, my students stay with me between six and nine months on average, coming once a week during the school year. In the summertime I offer camps with between 10–12 students who already know the basics of my program and simply keep their skills fresh over the summer months. My camps offer a lot of fun, competitive, and active skill building in an outdoor setting. The more fun my students have in my summer camps, the more they learn to enjoy the learning process itself. For most of them, learning during the school year is very hard and frustrating, and as a result a natural love of learning has never begun to develop for them. Syncing their learning to their OptiKode and bringing fun into the equation during the summer enables them to develop more love of learning.

WHY SOME PARENTS CONTINUE

I tell new clients, "I will move your student to grade level as quickly as possible, and once they get there I will let you know immediately." I truly don't want to keep students with me one minute longer than needed. In my mind, something is wrong if my students don't make steady and fairly rapid progress. I like for families to tell other families with struggling children how quickly their child got to grade level and how much fun he or she had in the process. However, it is not uncommon for parents to want to continue bringing their child to me even when they know that their child is on track and ready to end their work with me.

One father said that continuing to bring his son to me even though he no longer needed to was "an insurance policy." He would have paid any price, it seemed, to avoid seeing his son return to the state of anxiety and low self-esteem he exhibited at the end of kindergarten, which is when I first met this father. I did make good use of the additional time with his son, including helping him learn how to take his first standardized tests using an optisensory approach. The boy sailed through the tests and felt very confident, something that might have dented his new level of self-esteem had he not stayed that extra time with me.

Seeing parents worry about their child's continued progress after working with me has been a big part of my motivation in launching OptiKodes Academy on the Internet and making the website a place of ongoing support for families everywhere. As I hope you have come to see at this point, optisensory learners need to have their learning synced to their OptiKode every day of their school life for their skills to finally develop and be maintained. They need a stable, optisensory learning environment at home to ensure this happens. This is possible if parents take less than five hours out of their lives to learn the basics of the program and start using this student-centric program at home consistently.

Over time children get savvy about their OptiKode and come to see how they learn best. When this happens, they know how to use their Learning Shifts in middle school and beyond, but initially parent involvement is needed to jump start the process and bring a lasting Learning Shift to children at home. As I say to parents: you are already spending countless hours helping your child with their school work; why not do it in a way that will make all the difference for your child and your family relationships? Even your non-struggling children can be helped with the program. They, too, have an OptiKode that can be synced with the right tools and strategies, and that can reduce homework headaches and hassles that often exist between parents and children.

[10]

Kindergarten Readiness and OptiKodes

Kindergarten readiness is actually such a big topic that it warrants a separate book, but I will include a chapter here because so little is discussed and written about it. More should be available to help parents to make the right decision whether to wait an additional year before starting their child in school.

In a parent workshop I give, I discuss kindergarten readiness and show parents that there are three critical risk factors that should be thoroughly understood and considered before deciding whether a child is ready for kindergarten.

The three critical risk factors are:

- Is your child young for grade level?
- Is your child an optisensory learner?
- Does your child have learning disabilities?

RISK FACTOR 1—YOUNG FOR GRADE LEVEL

As I teach parents, if a child is young for grade level, that child should wait a year to begin kindergarten. Two years ago in California, the cutoff month rolled back from December to September. This means that if a student's birthday is in May or later, that child is at risk of falling behind and struggling due to being younger than many children in the class. Being four, five, or six months younger than one's peers does make a big difference in learning aptitude, and with reading instruction beginning so early in kindergarten, I recommend that parents with children who have May to September birthdays give their children one more year before beginning kindergarten.

Many parents resist this recommendation, feeling that their child will be bored if they wait another year. However, I have never seen an older child become bored in school. On the contrary, I see that older children become more naturally confident, are less susceptible to peer pressure in middle school, and become deeper thinkers who typically excel much more than the average student. I was such a student; being older never made me bored. I would finish my assigned work quickly and have time left to explore subjects more deeply and develop a highly academic mind.

I do think a lot of parents give in to the pressure of our overachievement society. Many of them succumb to our fast-track society and do not see that the greatest gift they can give their child is to not rush them into school before they are truly ready. I have never met a parent who has regretted giving their child that extra year. On the other hand, every parent I have met that has started their child early has regretted that decision a great deal. Once children begin school, it is very hard to turn back the clock and retain them.

Risk Factor 2—Student is Optisensory

If a parent answers "yes" to this question, it does not mean that your child should automatically wait another year. It does mean that your child is automatically at risk for underperformance because of the traditional teaching bias in the classroom discussed in this book. A "yes" to risk factor two means that your child will almost certainly struggle, and that you, as their parent, will go through a great deal of stress with them as a result. If you answer "yes" to both questions one and two, there is no doubt that you should wait another year before starting your child. The students in my practice who are both optisensory and young for their grade have the hardest time in the classroom. All optisensory learners struggle. The ones who are also on the young side struggle twice as hard.

RISK FACTOR 3—STUDENT HAS A LEARNING DISABILITY

Sometimes having a child who has one or more learning disabilities is enough to warrant giving a child an additional year. Especially with state standards being so accelerated nowadays, the presence of learning disabilities in today's fast-paced school curriculum justifies giving some learning-disabled students an additional year.

In my experience, children with disabilities seldom have just one disability. More often, they have several learning issues, which present considerable challenges. Often there are symptoms of anxiety or depression as well. Whether anxiety or depression stands on its own or results from school being difficult is hard to say. By the time learning disabilities are discovered, the child is in first or second grade and has already been struggling—enough time for these other mental health symptoms to set in if they weren't there from the beginning.

If a child has both risk factors two and three, I strongly recommend parents wait one more year. Being both optisensory and having disabilities is a double jeopardy. I can see no argument for throwing caution to the wind and setting a student—and their family—up for stress and defeat for every year of schooling thereafter.

Knowing these three risk factors can help parents navigate the all-important decision of when to start their child in kindergarten. Kindergarten readiness deserves serious consideration. I have been amazed over the years to see that general information about the risk factors for kindergarten are altogether missing from kindergarten registration days. That is where this information should show up and be made available to parents. At kindergarten registration most schools give a child a quick screening to see how many letter sounds and names they know. This is not even the tip of the iceberg when it comes to kindergarten readiness. The three risk factors above are what parents need to know to keep their kids from getting in over their heads, and then being blindsided when the kindergarten teacher informs them that their child is struggling at the first parent-teacher conference in December.

Parents may not be able to do anything about the traditional teaching bias in school, but they can make an informed decision about when and if their child is truly ready for kindergarten. Far too many parents have children with one or more risk factors who struggle throughout grade school.

It's the System, Not the Teacher

Public Education Is in Its Infancy

As a first step in thinking about reshaping our current educational system, it might be useful to ponder how long the system has been in place. National compulsory education began less than one hundred years ago, in 1918. The compulsory education movement began in the mid-1850s and got more popular over the next fifty years. By 1900, thirty-four states had compulsory schooling laws; of these, thirty had laws which required attendance until the age of fourteen, some even higher. The momentum towards compulsory education kept building. By 1910, 72% of American children attended school. Half of those children attended one-room schools. In 1918 every state in the U.S. required students to attend elementary school.

Ninety-five years is a very short run for any significant institution. When I was in elementary school in the mid–1960s, compulsory education had only been in place for fifty-three years! When I think about the system's lifespan in those personal terms, it feels to me like we were guinea pigs back then in a very young public school system. I think it's safe to say that we are only just now coming out of the system's infancy, and that the budget cuts, high dropout rates, and poor test results seen everywhere in the system are expressions of unavoidable growing pains in a young system shifting from the needs of the industrial revolution to the needs of the information age.

Reframing our understanding in such a way could make us more amenable to making changes which could empower each and every learner. This reframing would reason as follows:

- We have experimented and done a pretty good job with the first-ever compulsory public education system.
- We see that we've got the system about 60% right. Given the day and age we are in, a 100% success rate in the system is not only needed—it is possible!

When the first public education system was established and made mandatory, many Americans were still living on farms. However, we were quickly moving as a society into the industrial era, and a schooling system was needed to ensure that the population could read and write and handle life and jobs off the farm in an increasingly complex, non-agrarian country. The system that was devised was "standardized."

Cars, freeways, processed and canned foods, medical supplies, airplanes, ships, and clothing—everything was being mass-produced, and therefore the most productive and profitable factories were those that mastered the art of mass production and standardization. Is it any surprise then that the public school system became standardized too?

We live in a very different world today. Now, one century later, a lot has changed, yet our school system remains fundamentally the same. The focus is still on standardized learning, even though neuroscience and cognitive development research show our brains are multimodal. Amazingly, even though there are more schools, and computers are used in many of them, teaching methods are not much different today than those used in one-room school houses a hundred years ago.

New Times and New Solutions

Many of us have heard the current generation referred to as the "Information Age." I believe we have actually crossed over into a different age at this point, one I term the "Specialization Age." We are nothing now if not living in a finely-tuned, specialized world. We are living in a time where reliance on standardization and mass production is fading—we have become a highly specialized society and need the most specialized minds and systems to lead us into a safe and sane future. The OptiKodes System and all that it teaches supports the specialization of each learner's mind.

As I see it, the number and complexity of so many OptiKodes reflect the endless variations of creative minds and thinking. This results in an untold number of talents and abilities showing up in the course of human evolution.

We need to shift away from standardized education towards a system which empowers each learner's natural brilliance and abilities. OptiKodes gives us a key to unlock the brilliance of each learner and overcome the mind-numbing effects of standardized education on the unfolding genius of humankind. Standardized education is not in sync with the realities of our world. What is needed now is a new system that prepares specialized thinkers to bring new perspectives into the world. Instead of supporting specialized thinkers, today's outdated system is marginalizing great numbers of the brightest minds we have.

More than half of the children being left behind have OptiKodes similar to Albert Einstein and Steve Jobs. These learners have thinking- and moving-dominant OptiKodes and are capable of bringing forth life-changing theories and innovations. Yet each year by December of kindergarten, many of these learners who are reading-dormant are routinely disempowered and lose their connection with their innate brilliance. Their innovative, far-thinking minds are needed in the world. It is truly parents who hold the key to unlocking their children's abilities at home in a way that was never possible until now.

School Types, Ethnicities, and Socioeconomic Groups

It is important to point out that the misteaching epidemic I am describing knows no boundaries: it is present in all types of schools, in all income brackets, and in all ethnic groups. I often hear people express the belief that their child would not be struggling if they were in a private school with smaller class sizes. I dispel that belief right away and tell these parents that class size would not make a difference. I have students who attend private schools with only nine children in a class who are left behind and lose their love of learning as a result of the traditional curriculum that is being used in that private school.

I have yet to meet a single type of school that is truly multimodal and that uses all of the five modalities to effectively reach all the children in its classrooms. I have had struggling students come from Christian private schools, from Montessori-based elementary schools, and from other private but non-religious private schools. I have also had to help home-schooled children and students on independent study get to grade level with optisensory learning. The income brackets I serve range from the lower middle class to the very affluent. In most of these families at least one parent has attended college; sometimes both parents have advanced degrees.

In terms of ethnicity, I have helped children from Asian families, Hispanic families, African-American families, Persian families, and a cross section of other Middle Eastern families. The majority of my students, however, are from white, middle-class families who are very high-functioning and have spent a great deal of time and money during their children's early years to ensure they get a head start in school, including at least two years of attending preschool. Despite all of this, by kindergarten their children are routinely behind grade level in reading and are identified as struggling. Misteaching cuts across all known lines and affects children from all walks of life equally.

[12]

The Myth of Disabilities

ADD AND ADHD

This chapter may feel controversial, yet I believe that sharing what I know from experience about disabilities being "false culprits" for struggling students is a very important discussion to have with parents in my practice and readers of this book.

> Some professionals argue that ADHD is not truly a diagnostic disorder but rather the brain's adaptation to its perpetual exposure to multiple bits of information delivered through today's fast-paced technology. They contend that ADHD is not an illness but simply the result of new wiring patterns for the modern brain as it adapts to ever-present technology.
>
> —iBrain: Surviving the Technological Alteration of the Modern Mind, by Gary Small

As you might imagine, ADD and ADHD are the biggest suspects connected with underperformance in children. The common error in thinking is that moving-dominant students—usually boys—have ADHD. One can easily imagine why teachers jump to the conclusion that an overactive child who has a hard time sitting still has the disorder of focus and attention we call ADHD.

Here is an eye-opener: never once has a new student I've gotten whom a teacher thought had ADHD ever turned out to actually have this disorder. On the contrary, each year I do have a number of students who start optisensory learning with me who turn out to have ADD or ADHD. Somehow they have not hit the radar and go undiagnosed with this disorder.

What is going on here, when children with attention deficit are not diagnosed when they have it, and those that do not have the disorder are wrongly thought to have it? The answer to this question is this: attention deficit disorder is not as simple to understand and spot as you might think. To begin with, this disorder is a problem with attention—not activity—but we call it a hyperactivity disorder which ends up unnecessarily confusing people.

Kids with ADHD are not primarily hyperactive—they are primarily inattentive. What this points to is that students with the disorder have a very hard time keeping their minds in one place, much more so than their body. As I describe to parents in my practice, ADHD is a situation in which the mind is very, very overactive, so much so that it simply cannot rest in one place for more than a few seconds or so before it goes darting off in another direction. What is more, the places the mind travels between are often completely disconnected from each other and often seem very random.

Another thing I explain to parents to help them understand what it feels like to have ADHD is this: none of us has perfect attention. On any given day, a person without ADHD only has control of their attention between 65 and 85 percent of the time, I'd say. The rest of the time our attention "has a mind of its own" and we are not the captain of the ship during those minutes of our day.

A learner with ADHD, on the other hand, is very seldom able to control their attention like they need to and want to. I am willing to say that only about 20% of the time at best is a child with ADHD able to focus and maintain their attention as needed. That limited attentional ability causes a huge amount of interference for these children in every sphere of their lives, not just in school. Even when they know they need to pay attention and want to, children with ADHD or ADD simply cannot do so. For them it is rather like having an 8–track mind and never being able to keep the ball in the track which is needed given the task at hand. People without ADHD can put the ball in the track they want to and keep it there for as long as they need to focus and learn or to do something. Children with ADD or ADHD cannot, no matter how hard they try or what kind of consequences loom over them if they don't.

As you can imagine, it is a very anxiety-producing situation for a child to need to pay attention, to want to pay attention, but to be unable to pay attention. Some of this ongoing anxiety shows up for ADHD children as compulsive behavior. The world outside them is a demanding place where focus is prized above all else. Lacking this prized quality, the ADHD-affected child feels lost at sea and is constantly wondering when their ship will capsize. The low frustration tolerance and mood instability that is often seen in children with this disorder is largely connected to this predicament. It is safe to say that in a very real way, life is a living hell for these children, all of it connected to the balance of neurochemicals that produce good focus in most people, but not in the child with ADD or ADHD.

Another feature that shows up in children with ADHD is impulsivity. If one thinks about it for a moment, it makes sense that someone with a short attention span is not likely to be able to think through the consequences of their actions. Thinking something through carefully requires the ability to follow your own train of thought long enough to arrive at wise conclusions and sound judgments. Children with ADHD often don't have this kind of sustained thought process; they live and act "in the moment" and often do not connect the dots in a way that is possible for people without this disorder.

This same inability to track and focus also affects the social skills development of children with ADHD. Simply put, holding a conversation and attending to relationships requires an ability to focus on another person and to pick up their social cues. Sadly these children lack the requisite amounts of attention needed for social interaction and discourse, and often seem to withdraw into their own inner world and keep people at bay, or—as often happens—drive them away with inappropriate behavior. Often these children's personalities become rather introverted and disengaged as a result.

I have taken the time to reveal the inner world of a child with ADHD to help dispel the myth that this diagnosis is what is affecting the high-energy, kinetic children in the classroom and causing them to fall behind. It is not being hyperactive, but rather being robbed of their need to channel their high energy into learning that derails these other moving-dominant children.

I hope after revealing more about the nuances of ADHD, that you can see the active child through a completely different lens. The active child in the classroom is just that—active—but seldom do they have a deficit of attention. The problem with their learning is that they are being made to sit still in chairs far longer than their body can tolerate. This disengages them from learning. It can easily lead a frustrated teacher to wrongly conclude that ADHD is in play for such a student.

The active child is usually one with a moving-dominant OptiKode who absolutely must be aligned with their strong kinetic energy to learn. Sitting still for too long literally causes these learners' attention and focus to plummet. These learners reenergize and can stay engaged longer when they are allowed to use movement and moderate amounts of activity to learn. When they start working with me, using study intervals and active learning games, they bring laser-like focus to what they are learning. A child with ADHD would be incapable of this kind of focus.

Each year I write several reports to teachers educating them about the needs of the moving-dominant learner and recommending ways they can support them with more active learning strategies in the classroom. I know teachers want nothing more than to reach their students and develop a trusting relationship with them.

UNDERDIAGNOSING ADD AND ADHD

Every year in my practice, I have a couple of students whom I suspect have ADD or ADHD. Remarkably, the possibility of their having attention deficit has gone completely "under the radar" until I bring it up. The problem, of course, is that this is a very debilitating disorder if it is not diagnosed and treated, and yet many doctors don't want to prescribe medication, even if they have diagnosed it.

I don't want to imply that this failure to prescribe is true with all doctors or pediatricians who diagnose attention deficit, but occasionally I do have to push hard to get a doctor to prescribe a trial of medication, which invariably makes a huge improvement in a student and their learning abilities.

Recently, at the end of this last academic year, I wrote a report for a student who was finishing his junior year. After working with him for several months, I began to suspect that he had ADD. When I brought this up with his mother she indicated that she had been considering the same thing. This student is one of the hardest-working students I have ever had. A star athlete at his school, he would come home from basketball practice or lacrosse or cross-country tournaments and put in several hours of work each night. He also set aside additional time to study for tests and came to me weekly for academic support. However, try as he might, he was not getting the grades that a traditional student would have gotten with so much effort.

Because he was not making better grades, I knew that there was something more than just being optisensory that was interfering with his learning process. After four months of working with him in an optisensory way, I felt he should have been showing more improvement. I came to suspect that he was one of the students with ADD going under the radar, one of the students not being diagnosed and helped with medication. His doctor agreed to a trial of medication, and now three months into his senior year, he is doing much better and is freed of the anxiety that overwhelmed him last year. As controversial as medication is for this disorder, I have seen it serve as a complete life-changer for every student who has begun taking it. I know how fearful parents can be when faced with the decision whether to medicate or not, but never once has a parent in my practice regretted their decision to do so. Just the opposite, many have felt very guilty for having waited so long to do the one thing that made a complete difference in their child's ability to focus and excel in school.

Here is an excerpt from a report to a doctor for the student I referred to above who is now a senior in high school:

My Observations and Recommendations

In working with "A," I see a student who is inattentive and often skims the surface of what he is discussing or working on with me. He has a clear desire to engage and succeed in school and his work, but he often seems "dreamy" and not quite present in our sessions. Given how inattentive he is while working one-on-one with me, I can only imagine how much more inattentive he is when he is working independently at home or in the classroom. He reports a chronic inability to focus in class during lectures, at home while studying, and also during test-taking. The frustration, stress and worry that is developing is significantly interfering with his state of mind, and I see symptoms of an anxiety disorder taking hold in him.

"A" is a student who wishes to attend college and to participate in a sports program there. He is experiencing overwhelming levels of anxiety as a result of struggling with sustaining attention, and his motivation and hope of ever getting into college is plummeting. From everything that I and his parents observe and he reports, a diagnosis for attention deficit should be considered and a trial of medication started. The summer months will be a good time to see if medication will enable him to focus and help him to engage in learning more optimally. I will be working with him over the summer and will be able to help his parents monitor the efficacy of the medication on his learning, functioning, and self-esteem.

I want to point out that this was a case of attention deficit that went unnoticed until the student in question was already at the end of his junior year and beginning to go into a rapid downward spiral of anxiety. His dream of playing college basketball was fading because his grades were not high enough to get into the colleges he was aiming for. His mother reported the anxious meltdowns he went through around college testing time. He was losing interest in applying himself his last year of high school. In short, this student had reached his breaking point. Being an optisensory learner was hard enough. Not getting the help that I believe every student with attention deficit deserves—including pharmacological help—was the last straw. Although this teen got the help he deserved, many other children and teens are being left to drift off and be sucked into the preventable undertow of attention deficit. I am not arguing for a return to the days of overmedication and a rush to diagnosis, but this is an important topic which definitely warrants more open discussion and parent education.

UNDERSTANDING DYSLEXIA

Another false culprit used to explain the high rate of underperformance in students is dyslexia. I can imagine how easy it would be if I were a teacher, and not a learning specialist, to think that dyslexia is a prime cause of so much delayed learning in students. Optisensory learners who are not offered multimodal reading and learning strategies in the classroom have been turned upside down in their learning process. In other words, without the right reading program ever being offered them, their whole reading foundation is shaky. By the time they get to me and I assess them, they have gaping holes in all skill areas. They leave out words and sometimes drop whole lines as they read; they sound choppy; they guess at words rather than systematically decoding them; and their comprehension is very poor, to name just some of their deficits. Teachers see symptoms such as these and make the leap to dyslexia as the underlying problem.

I have had many students with dyslexia in my practice over the years. In my experience with these students, however, their dyslexic symptoms are far less disruptive to their learning than their being an optisensory student stuck in a classroom where standardized teaching methods are biased toward reading-dominant students. Most of us think that dyslexia is a chronic syndrome in which many of the words on a page in front of the student are moving around for them and making things a visual nightmare to read. I can assure you this is just not the case. What happens instead is what I refer to as "occasional dyslexic moments." What I mean by this is that for the average dyslexic student, there is one moment every couple of pages or so when two letters in a single word reverse themselves or perhaps disappear and then reappear. Most students have a single visual abnormality or pattern that shows up for them—either a tendency for letters to reverse, disappear or sometimes momentarily duplicate in the white space above.

But these visual anomalies do not occur frequently enough to really be the underlying cause for a child's learning delays. Rather, as I have argued throughout this book, it is being a child who has needed optisensory reading techniques from day one of kindergarten, but who has not gotten them, that underlies so many learning difficulties in these children. In my professional experience, being an optisensory learner in a traditional classroom is the most disabling learning factor any child faces.

I want to reinforce this last message by adding that almost half of the children who come to me have known learning disabilities. Often they have had years of treatment for disorders such as hearing and visual processing deficits, eye-teaming and motor-sensory integration problems, pragmatic language deficits, Asperger's, low developmental IQ, and lastly ADD or ADHD. The crux of the matter though is this: even when their other disorders have been treated, these children are still behind and struggling. Only when they embark on the OptiKodes program with me do they get on track and truly begin to thrive.

BENEFITS FOR THE LEARNING DISABLED

Another category of student with disabilities—one who is a traditional learner, yet learning disabled—can benefit from the OptiKodes System. The precision and custom fit of optisensory learning can help compensate, in part, for some disabilities. Let me give you an example:

A mother of a young girl who had a profound hearing loss met me in a local grocery store. Her daughter was bright but had a significant hearing loss which was interfering with her learning to read in kindergarten. I assessed her daughter's OptiKode and saw that her reading was dominant and that she was a traditional learner. Nevertheless, her hearing disability was getting in the way of her gaining early reading skills and confidence in her learning abilities. Using her OptiKode, I knew exactly how to teach this child in a way that went right around the hearing loss and targeted the other two dominant modalities. This child caught fire like any other optisensory learner. She has just started third grade, and her mother reports she has been at the top of her class the last three years and loves school and learning.

I could tell you many, many more stories like this from within my student population. My message is this: children with disabilities who sync their learning with their OptiKode more effectively overcome the interference that comes from their particular disabilities.

I don't want to suggest that parents stop taking their children to good specialists when they have been diagnosed with disabilities. I am saying, though, that the OptiKodes System will generally help reduce the amount of time and money needed and increase results. For those with simple learning delays, OptiKodes will be sufficient and you will not in fact need further resources. I have seen this many times. Children with diagnosed disabilities such as auditory processing, dyslexia, and pragmatic language deficits are given optisensory learning, and it has done the trick. Depending on your child's situation and learning difficulty, OptiKodes may be the complete answer. For more learning-disabled children, OptiKodes will be one of several interventions that your child needs to quickly and more cost effectively reach their full potential.

[13]

Modern Times, Modern Problems

FACING EXTINCTION: HANDWRITING

Very few people are aware of what is happening with handwriting in school these days. The changes that word processing and keyboards are bringing into our lives is rapidly bringing about a deterioration of students' ability to write. Cursive handwriting is taking a huge beating and, in my opinion, there will likely be a time in the not-too-distant future when cursive handwriting itself will no longer be included in the Common Core Standards.

The trends I see that are unhinging students' ability to acquire strong and long lasting handwriting skills:

- Most of my students in fourth through twelfth grade have very poor penmanship.
- Starting in fourth grade, students are required to use keyboarding skills. Some teachers in the districts near me are moving towards asking for more typed assignments by fourth-grade students.

Here is one of three Common Core Standards related to the "production and distribution of writing:"

CCSS.ELA-Literacy.W.4.6 With some guidance and support from adults, use technology, including the Internet, to produce and publish writing as well as to interact and collaborate with others; demonstrate sufficient command of keyboarding skills to type a minimum of one page in a single sitting.

⑤ Will Common Core Kill Education? → optiko.de/2k

I find it amazing that nine- and ten-year-olds in fourth grade are being asked to know how to type a one-page document in a single sitting. Would it surprise anyone to know that it is often parents who typically do the typing, not their children? Ultimately, not only are children getting less of the critical writing experience they need, but they themselves are not getting keyboarding experience either—their parents are typing assignments for them. Editing and thinking skills are failing to develop for children as a result.

There is a window of time for the development of handwriting, which I see closes sometime between the seventh and eighth grade. After that time helping students improve their penmanship and spelling is almost impossible. Gone are the days when students spent countless hours perfecting their cursive handwriting.

Cursive is begun in third grade, but a very cursory attempt is put into it over the course of that year. Students only need to demonstrate a minimal proficiency with cursive in the first months of fourth grade. Once they "demonstrate that they can produce it," however crudely, they are then given the option to revert to hand printing letters, if they prefer. Needless to say, most children revert to hand printing instead of cursive.

Very few children in grades four to twelve can read cursive. The handwriting of most middle school and high school students resembles that of a student at least four to five years younger than their actual grade level. Illegibility and messiness is the norm for 95% of the handwriting samples I see.

I tell parents that they are the last defense in making sure their child acquires solid handwriting skills that will last them a lifetime. I warn parents that they can have the brightest student on the block, but their child will still have to do handwritten essays when they sit for college entrance exams. Keyboards are not yet provided to students when they have to do the written response section of those timed exams. Messy, illegible, and poorly-spelled written essays will not get teens the high scores they need to get into the colleges of their choice.

One final issue worth addressing has to do with the eye-hand-brain connection which gets activated when longhand writing is used. Studies show that when students write by hand, they make unique connections and think more creatively than when they type on a keyboard. Something vital seems to get lost when kids sit down and type without writing their first drafts by hand. Are we willing to accept Common Core Standards when they veer away from this important goal: cultivating deep and creative thinkers who are connected to their thinking process in meaningful ways?

I hope as this section ends that you will walk away and think twice about your role in protecting the development of your children's basic handwriting abilities. There will be time enough in the years to come for them to keyboard. Hold the line and ensure they do their papers by hand. Let their teachers know how much you value them acquiring the ability to write as an important, lifelong skill.

READING ASSESSMENT PRESSURES

Lexia Reading is a computerized reading program that provides phonics instruction and gives students independent practice in basic reading skills. Lexia Reading is designed to supplement regular classroom instruction. It is designed to support skill development in the five areas of reading instruction identified by the National Reading Panel.

Two studies of Lexia Reading meet What Works Clearinghouse (WWC) evidence standards. One study meets WWC evidence standards with reservations. The three studies included 314 students in kindergarten and first grade in two states. Based on these three studies, the WWC considers the extent of evidence for Lexia Reading to be small for alphabetics, fluency, comprehension, and general reading achievement.

Lexia Reading was found to have potentially positive effects on alphabetics, no discernible effects on fluency, potentially positive effects on comprehension, and no discernible effects on general reading achievement.

The What Works Clearinghouse (WWC) was established in 2002 as an initiative of the Institute for Education Sciences (IES) at the U.S. Department of Education. The WWC is administered by the National Center for Education Evaluation within IES.

🐦 What Works Clearinghouse—Lexia Reading ➜ optiko.de/2z

Lexile Scoring Can Stifle Students

Each year as school resumes, a couple of things invariably jump out and get my attention. Just today a student came into my office and shared "some news" as we were saying our hellos and getting the session started. She shared with me that she learned what her "Lexile score" was. I had not heard this term before so I asked her to explain what it was. "Lexile" is a term that her school uses to describe a student's reading level. She learned that she is a level 868—a score that apparently was at grade level. Her 868 score is right where it was at the end of last year when summer began. I could hear that she was somewhat disappointed that her Lexile had not increased over the summer. As we talked more, I felt a growing unease. What is wrong with a school system that starts leveling students' reading abilities beginning in elementary school and shares this information on a regular basis so it is known to students every day of their academic lives?

This situation regarding my student's Lexile score is simply the tip of the iceberg floating in a sea of other pieces of feedback I am getting from parents. At the top of the list is this reading leveling phenomenon. It is barely three weeks into the new school year, and children and parents already know their exact reading level. What's more, my optisensory students know that the traditional students are way out in front of them in the class. These traditional children set the bar very high for everyone and are easily 6–12 months ahead of grade level in reading, but are seen as the norm for the class. Compared to this, many students feel behind, when in fact they are at or slightly above grade level. As I said to my student today, I don't think it is right for this leveling system to be shared with students. The harmful effects this causes for many students include:

- being overly anxious about their performance
- constantly comparing themselves to other students' progress
- feeling that grade level standards are not satisfactory—promoting compulsive overachievement on one end and self-denigration on the other
- focusing children away from the intrinsic enjoyment of learning towards trying to measure up to competitive standards
- fostering unkind competition
- engendering jealousy and frustration
- causing many children to give up and hate school.

This leveling system results in each student being told what book level they should read in when they select books. The mother of a third grade student of mine, Jimmy, shared with me that she was informed that her son's reading level was 2.6–3.8. This was good news—this range shows that he is actually above grade level (he is in third grade). The bad news is that this leveling system can unnecessarily restrict children to a prescribed grade level spread. Children might feel discouraged from reading a book above their assessed grade level spread.

I don't think this kind of restriction is good for children. They should be free to stretch themselves and see how far they can go. I remember as a child finding out that I was able to read *Charlotte's Web* well before my teacher or parents thought I was able to. My teacher was thrilled one day to find me reading it at my desk. She beamed from ear to ear and congratulated me on being such a capable reader. How would I have responded if she had told me to switch books, because *Charlotte's Web* was above my level and not right for me?

It has to also be said that this leveling system requires regular testing of students. I know because parents routinely bring in their worry that their child is slipping behind, and I have to constantly reassure them that things are fine. All of this brings about a chronic fixation on assessments and leveling, and ultimately creates students who don't really know what the reading process is all about, so much as whether their level is going up or down.

A student of mine today explained that she has to read a book each week and test out on it on the computer. This happens in many of the local elementary schools. While it keeps certain children from falling through the cracks, it is creating a generation of kids who are stressed out of their minds about the leveled, test-based approach to reading that exists in most classrooms. We are creating "test takers," not thinkers.

Schoolchildren's mental health and well being as well as their orientation towards learning itself is becoming alarmingly skewed. Children and their parents are becoming overly focused on assessments. They are more interested in test scores than what books are meant to bring young readers: an understanding and appreciation of the world and one's place in it.

It is hard to trace the origins of all of this overachievement, but our tolerance for it has dire consequences. One powerful new documentary film, *Race to Nowhere,* shows how the stress of school life negatively affects most students in our country. It reveals how teen depression and suicide rates are at an all-time high, and how much of this is related to overwhelming school stress. I recommend to all the parents in my practice that they watch this film, and I recommend everyone reading this book do the same. As I write this book, France is currently moving towards making homework illegal. Teachers in France are already prohibited from giving homework on weekends and holidays. Will the U.S. follow suit and take steps to keep homework from hijacking our students' mental health and many families' well being?

Race To Nowhere (film) → optiko.de/30

Technology—The Good, the Bad, and the Ugly

I am personally a big fan of using things like YouTube, smartphones, and educational apps of all kinds in my work with students. I show parents how to guide their students to places like SparkNotes, YouTube, Dictionary.com, and iTranslate. At SparkNotes a student can get a summary of a particular literature classic before he or she starts reading it for class. Most students read Shakespeare in either ninth or tenth grade nowadays—a year or two before we did in past generations—and getting the plot and characters landed with SparkNotes can make all the difference in whether a student will turn on to Shakespeare or not.

A student of mine who is a senior at a private high school was assigned *Frankenstein* by Mary Shelley at the beginning of the school year. Even though his English teacher had discussed the book and plot with the class, he started reading the book with very little understanding of the context or storyline. This is not an unusual situation for optisensory learners—they need to engage themselves actively in learning, and hearing a teacher's overview can feel passive to such a student. Once we discussed the overview of *Frankenstein* in Spark Notes in a way he could relate to, he was a lot more interested in reading the story.

I am becoming more interested in the options for enhancing learning for optisensory learners each year with student-friendly, online resources. For many years now, my students have been keeping me up to date with new apps and learning tools they find, and they often teach me things about my iPhone I wouldn't otherwise learn. Just the other day one of my second-grade students showed me how to undo a problem on my iPhone that I could not figure out how to undo myself. The point is that students' lives are filled with electronic devices of all kinds, and they are totally invested in using them. My feeling is that it just makes good sense to find ways to use their love affair with electronic devices to aid them in learning—in other words, meet them on their playing field and excite greater interest and passion in their learning with their smartphones, iPods, Kindles, tablets, and laptops.

Myths and Misconceptions of Technology in the Classroom

Though computers and technology are playing a greater role in learning and in the classroom, we need to ask, "Is all of this added technology improving learning outcomes and students' abilities?" An even more fundamental question: "Is it wise to use technology to reinforce the standardized system that inherently leaves so many children on the sidelines as a matter of course?"

Unfortunately, today's obsession with computer technology and video gaming appears to be stunting frontal lobe development in many teenagers, impairing their social and reasoning abilities. If young people continue to mature in this fashion, their brains' neural pathways may never catch up. It is possible that they could remain at an immature and self-absorbed emotional level, right through adulthood.

—iBrain: Surviving the Technological Alteration of the Modern Mind, by Gary Small

I think there is an argument to be made for applying technology in the service of revamping the system as we know it instead of reinforcing the old system now in place. When a system is inherently flawed, is it best to patch things up with technology that masks the problem, or find wholly new solutions? I do not like using technology in a manner which inevitably supports the traditional teaching bias in classrooms. More and more of the time, students are reading on computers rather than from textbooks. Increasingly, I am hearing my students report that they are doing their regular reading labs and the related tests on computers. Are we correct in our assumption that these computers are aiding students' learning and test-taking skills?

Research is showing that reading on ebooks is not improving students' abilities. In fact, findings show that:

- Students' reading rate is noticeably slower when they read electronically, by as much as 20–30%.
- When reading on screens, students need to read repetitively for information to be fully imparted to them and to stick. One reason this seems to be so is that reading electronically does not offer the same physical placement cues that help our minds locate, store, and retrieve information. A handheld book that we can flip back and forth through concretely activates this storage and retrieval element of our memory, something that electronic screens do not make possible.

🐦 Do E-Books Impair Memory? ➜ optiko.de/31

Reading to young children from screens like iPads is less effective in helping them with early reading skills development. It appears that iPads distract children with the gaming features that they know reside on the device, and that parents tend to stop and talk less with their children about the story when they are reading from an electronic device.

Yet another good article gives five compelling reasons why a handheld book is superior to an electronic screen any day of the week—read it when you have ten minutes in which you want to have your mind opened to the dangers of rushing to replace books with electronic reading.

🐦 5 Reasons Books Are Better Than E-Books ➜ optiko.de/32

To be fair-minded, do read an article from the opposing side of this argument which gives five benefits of using screens to read.

🐦 5 Ways That eBooks Are Better Than Paper Books ➜ optiko.de/33

When all is said and done, I come down on the side of feeling that computers and technology will not be the solution to our ailing school system. A wholesale change is needed.

More Thoughts On Common Core

Any parent or educator nowadays is well aware of the latest overhaul in our education system: Common Core. It is not a new teaching approach or system, but rather a new set of standardized tests that are aimed at making sure middle and high school students are meeting clear baselines in math and reading. This might all sound well and good, except that companies that produce and sell teaching materials are marketing their materials as "Common Core aligned." Many critics of establishing this new Common Core national standard say it is simply a backdoor way of nationalizing curriculum to sell books and materials.

This is especially alarming given the fact that the new Common Core standards were created by a small group of private individuals in Washington, DC without input from teachers or parents. No studies or pilot tests were ever done. How is it that a small group of individuals were able to so quickly push through this new set of testing standards to almost every state without more rigorous testing or involving educators? As a reading of the full story will reveal:

> "In fact, the only mathematician and the only ELA expert on the validation committee refused to sign off on the standards because they are inadequate," she added, "Yet, the standards have been copyrighted and cannot be changed, and this is resulting in a loss of local and state control."

As for how teachers are feeling about Common Core, a recent article reveals how many educators are feeling about the new standards:

> "A growing number of teachers say the national standards, adopted by some forty-five states, have combined with pressure to "teach to the test" to take all individuality out of their craft. Some teachers told FoxNews.com the new education approach is turning their lessons into little more than data-dispensing sessions, and they fear their jobs are being marginalized."

🖲 Teachers complain Common Core-linked lessons little more than scripts to read ➜ optiko.de/34

In my mind the impact of Common Core will only be to worsen the situation for nontraditional students in classrooms everywhere. I am already seeing them cause more stress and strain for my optisensory learners, who must contend with more rigid and fast-paced, reading-dominant curriculum in their classrooms at every grade level.

[14]

Learning for Everyone

THE OPTIKODES CLASSROOM

I recently described my vision of an OptiKode classroom to my father, who as I mentioned earlier, is an optisensory learner. Like many nontraditional learners, my father did not go on to college. He has the OptiKode of an artist, because his seeing modality is most dominant in his code. I think his life would have turned out very differently if he had known how to use his OptiKode throughout his life. His recent question to me was, "What would a classroom look like if it weren't standardized and was geared towards optisensory learning?" That got me off and running to share my vision with him of how optisensory learning could transform classrooms everywhere.

The OptiKodes classroom would not be set up uniformly with twenty or more chairs facing forward to support the "sit, look, and listen" approach.

THE MOVING-DOMINANT ZONE

One quarter of the class would be the Moving-Dominant Zone—MDZ—for those students with moving-dominant OptiKodes. In this section, there would

be stability balls to sit on and clipboards to use as temporary desks. The balls could be used in a variety of ways to enable students to be in motion while learning. It is critical for students with moving-dominant OptiKodes to be active learners. Without activity, these students rapidly lose focus and interest. BodyPlusLearning techniques would be emphasized in this active learning zone. The MDZ would also have:

- Stand-up dry-erase easels where students could stand and do class work instead of staying seated
- Portable easels that could be moved around within the active zone as needed or desired
- Ample wall space with mounted dry erase boards and chalkboard walls offering "writing walls" for students to engage both their gross motor and fine motor skills while learning
- An area where students could pace around in circles or "walking paths" as they thought over lessons or read—yes, reading while walking is an effective technique for moving-dominant learners
- A large and varying selection of different markers and colored chalk, which would be available for use on the writing walls. A variety of tactile inputs is very helpful for moving-dominant learners. The essential thing in the active zone would be honoring the natural kinetic learning energy of students and helping them tap into it for optimal productivity.
- A few wall-mount basketball hoops and soft balls to take shots while working and during stimulation breaks. Other indoor physical activities like magnetized darts would also be available. Whereas parents and teachers fear that kids will lose productivity if those sorts of games are on hand, moving-dominant learners are really able to self-regulate and use them

to keep focused and productive—parent volunteers can help monitor the times students do lose focus.

THE HEARING-DOMINANT ZONE

One quarter of the classroom would be designated the Hearing-Dominant Zone—HDZ. In this area verbal exchange and discussion would be emphasized. Students would be drawn there because of their hearing-dominant OptiKodes. These are the learners who learn best by talking—not just by listening, which is the default in most classrooms. Here are some of the features of the HDZ:

- iPods or headsets connected to a music source would be available so that children could listen to music while learning.
- WhisperPhones so students can hear themselves read better—these devices enhance learning for hearing-dominant students. The music selection would be varied to assist students in learning which kinds of music help them in different subject areas.
- The HDZ would greatly benefit from parent volunteer support. Children who are hearing-dominant simply cannot cement their learning without verbally expressing their understanding out loud. Parent volunteers could spend time in this zone inviting students to verbalize and integrate what they are learning.
- Parent volunteers in this zone could also take groups of students outside the classroom for even more robust talking in small groups or individually with one student at a time.
- ⓥ WhisperPhone➜ optiko.de/35

THE THINKING-DOMINANT ZONE

Another quarter of the classroom would be set up as the Thinking-Dominant Zone—TDZ. Among other things, in this section volunteers would help students create a

study plan for the work they needed to do. This breaking down of a project into systematic steps helps thinking students thrive. Also included in this zone would be:

- Timers for students to set a series of alarms that would signal when to take short breaks and when to resume working. This kind of structured learning approach, with timed intervals, works well for thinking learners.
- The TDZ would be where students would go to work on the math and science curriculum. There would be a variety of calculators, visual aids for math, and parent volunteers who have strong math skills.
- During their short activity breaks, students from this zone could spend five minutes in the moving-dominant zone where they could throw a few soft balls into a wall mounted basketball hoop or play a game of magnetized darts with another learner who is on break. Or they could spend time in the hearing-dominant zone talking with a volunteer about what they have just learned.

Remember, students have three or four dominant intelligences in their OptiKodes, and although a student might start a work session in the thinking-dominant zone, he or she might travel to the hearing-dominant zone next, and then to the moving-dominant zone last depending on what their personal OptiKode is. Even traditional learners who are reading-dominant have two or three other dominant intelligences in their OptiKodes. Although they are not the students who struggle, they too would benefit immensely by having their overall school day synced to their OptiKode and traveling around the various OptiKode zones in a classroom.

THE SEEING-DOMINANT ZONE

The Seeing-Dominant Zone—SDZ—would be filled with visual tools and techniques which would help the students with visually dominant OptiKodes. The use of Quick Pics would be central in this zone. Students would storyboard a writing assignment they had to do before writing to get their ideas formed and sequenced before sitting down to write. Quick Pics also are invaluable for reading comprehension and vocabulary development. The seeing-dominant zone would also include:

- Stand-up dry-erase easels to make large Quick Pics, or 3x5 card decks that come with all sorts of colorful covers
- If a student uses a dry erase board or easel to make their Quick Pics, they could take a picture of their work when finished. It could be saved and used later in the classroom or sent home, depending on their grade level and whether work at home with the Quick Pix would need to be continued.
- Parent volunteer support in the zone would facilitate the use of YouTube to retrieve videos that would help a student with a task at hand—maybe learning more about the American Revolution or something on the California Missions. Optisensory students simply learn better by seeing and hearing information rather than reading about it exclusively in a textbook.

Each student's OptiKode tells us exactly which way they learn best. The kind of classroom I am describing would give each learner a way to sync up their learning in these four zones each and every day of school.

In such an OptiKodes classroom, all the Common Core Standards would still be taught, but in a way that reached every eager mind in the room. Students would quickly come to know what their OptiKode is, how to travel between learning zones in the classroom, and how to sync learning to their code. The fundamental change would be away from whole-group teaching towards short teaching units, and then sending students off into the right zones to ensure they integrate the teaching according to their OptiKode.

Parent volunteers would be trained to assist with this process, which would be a great use of their support. As it is now, parents as a group contribute many, many hours of classroom support each year. Instead of continuing to reinforce standardized learning, this new paradigm would use parent help in setting up and running these OptiKode zones and exciting children's interest and learning in radically new ways. Such a classroom is not an outlandish vision, nor would it be hard to implement. The only question is: are we ready for change or not? Are we truly committed to engaging the full learning potential of each child?

How Interval Studying Creates Better Students

Another benefit of the OptiKodes System is that it can show learners what kind of breaks to take during study periods. Learning breaks can be done in alignment with a student's OptiKode, which then helps them be more productive when they return to studying.

As a first step in talking about breaks, let's start by considering what it is we actually need when we take a break from studying or work. When students tire and need a break, they experience lowered mental focus and physical energy. In those moments they feel tapped out and need a break to recharge their system before returning to work.

> ...the truth is that well-credentialed educational theorists had long before determined that ten to eighteen minutes was about the limit of students' attention spans.
>
> —The One World Schoolhouse, Salman Khan

I have been very curious over the years why it is that students and even adults lose stamina and need breaks. Why can't students study easily without breaks until a project is complete? After all, the synapses in our brains fire continuously and are ever-ready for us to use in the service of our learning or working needs. So why do we tire out and need to stop?

I believe that we tire out as quickly as we do because we are not using all of our brain's five modalities equally, but instead typically overuse one or two modalities at a time. In other words, we over-amp a few areas of our brain, rather than distributing the learning load equally across all hemispheres of learning.

What happens to an electrical system when too much energy runs through the circuits? As we have all experienced in our homes, the breaker switch gets thrown, which shuts down the whole electrical system in the house. I believe this is essentially what happens when students overtax one or two modalities while studying—they run too much energy through a certain area in their brain, which overloads and tires them out prematurely. At that point a break is needed to reboot the system and get their mental energy flowing more uniformly through their brain's circuitry.

I believe that if we supported children to learn in a more balanced, multimodal way, they would have more endurance and would not feel as drained and tapped out at the end of a study period. I also feel there would be a lot more enjoyment and satisfaction at the heart of learning itself as a result.

What would a more balanced approach to learning look like? It is something I use routinely with my students and call "interval studying." With interval studying at home, students study in 15–40 minute cycles (depending on their age) and change their study location at the end of each cycle. This integrates core principles of my Body-PlusLearning program. They also use different elements such as more audio input—music or verbal discussion; more visual input—

YouTube videos and other online media; and create a study plan each day which involves using a preset timer on their phone—a thinking strategy. I use this kind of interval studying during each hour-long session with my students. The intervals I use in my practice run between eight and twelve minutes. After two or three intervals I always have the student take a "stimulation break."

A stimulation break is just as it sounds: it is downtime that is meant to recharge and enliven the student's mind. Often we think of breaks as a time to "veg out," but this is not at all what a stimulation break should accomplish. The aim of a stimulation break is to have students do something fun that aligns with their dominant modalities. What this ends up providing for the student is a perfect attunement to the energy available in their dominant intelligences. This attunement gives them a feeling of harmonic resonance and brings about what many of us have heard described as a flow state. If you have ever "gotten lost" while doing something pleasurable and have completely forgotten the passage of time and even that you are present, you know how pleasurable a flow state can be. Experiencing this flow state for even a few minutes can reboot and recalibrate a student such that they are able to resume working with a fresh mind at the end of their break.

Without interval studying and taking the right kinds of stimulation breaks, students are at half-mast at best in their productivity before the first hour of homework is even finished. This does not bode well for high school students, who typically have several hours of homework most nights. Overtaxed students are running on fumes and cannot possibly be bringing vital thinking and interest to their studies.

On the other end of the spectrum, children in early elementary school are overwhelmed and stressed out. Because interval studying and stimulation breaks are so essential for all students, I teach parents how to design both of them well for their children in the Opti-

Kodes training. Parents become very enthused when they learn how to match their child's OptiKode to the right interval studying methods and stimulation breaks. Every parent sincerely wants to learn how to support their child better. The techniques for interval studying and stimulation breaks are complete deal changers in the homes of parents who have learned how to implement them successfully.

How OptiKodes Can Help You Pick the Right Books for Your Child

One of the most critical reading issues for optisensory learners is matching them with the books which will interest them and make reading fun for them. Because of how mismatched classroom reading methods are for these students, their reading skills fail to develop adequately beginning in kindergarten. As a result, their interest in reading is nothing like that of traditional learners. They avoid reading because it is hard for them and almost never enjoyable. While these learners do like being read to at home and by teachers in class, picking up a book and reading is usually the last thing they like to do. In the rare times these learners pick out a book, they seldom know how to go about finding one that will match their interests and reading level.

The thing that can change this predicament for optisensory learners is to help them understand what kinds of books they like and how to easily find those books at home, school, bookstores, and at libraries. The sooner parents can identify and match the right books with their child, the better chance their child has to begin to enjoy reading. Reading time translates into better reading skills—it's as simple as that.

By the end of high school, there is a huge disparity between the number of books a traditional learner has read and the number an optisensory learner has completed. Traditional learners, who generally read well and enjoy it, will find the time to do additional reading. They typically read many more books than are assigned to them in their classes at school. Traditional learners also seem to like a cross-section of genres and have diverse reading interests. By contrast, optisensory learners usually have a much narrower range of books they like, almost never read more than what is assigned them.

If parents start early enough matching the right kinds of books with their children and help them learn to read in an optisensory way, they will develop a wider interest in reading different kinds of books and likely develop a genuine love of reading. The secret to matching nontraditional children with the right genres lies in knowing their OptiKode. Here is how it works: whatever lies in the top two placements of a child's OptiKode points to the types of books they will naturally like reading.

Examples:

- In a child's OptiKode where the first placement is moving and the second is thinking—the child will like action packed books (Moving #1), especially if there is something to figure out in the story (Thinking #2). Spy novels, detective stories, mysteries, and science fiction with a lot of action will interest this child and be a good fit.

- In a child's OptiKode where the first placement is hearing and the second is seeing—the child will like books which are loaded with characters that use a lot of dialogue (Hearing #1) and where the scenes throughout the book are vividly described (Seeing #2). An added plus for this child will be if the book is filled with pictures. These children will create voices spontaneously for all the

characters as they read and will create a stream of scenes in their minds. Doing this will keep them fully engaged in the reading experience and will be highly enjoyable.

- In a child's OptiKode where the first placement is thinking and the second is moving—the child will be drawn to books where he or she can figure out things and learn a lot (Thinking #1). In the early grades books like *The Magic Tree House* and *The Magic School Bus* will interest this child a lot. Books that investigate the animal kingdom, dinosaurs, bats, polar bears, and other things in the natural world will also be of interest to this kind of learner.

The examples above are not a full list of the kinds of pairings that match children's OptiKodes with the right high-interest books for them, but I hope you see how to approach the book selection process from this perspective. An OptiKodes workshop will help you determine precisely which books are the best fit for your child and increase the likelihood that they will become more engaged readers. Once you know the type of books that align with your child, you are ready to do an OptiKode book sort that generates more excitement when choosing books with your child.

OptiKode Book Sort

Take five to ten books from the genre identified by the OptiKode and spread them out on the floor in front of your child. Be sure you are both in a good mood and you are not rushed for time. Using the third example above to show you how to do an OptiKode book sort, have an assortment of books from the *Magic Tree House* series, a few from the *Magic School Bus* series, and four or five other selections from the realm of science and nature. Then proceed as follows:

1. Tell your child that he or she will create three book piles from all the books laid out in front of them.

2. The pile on the left will be their "low interest pile," the pile in the middle will be their "medium interest pile," and the pile on the right will be their "high interest pile."

3. Instruct your child to take at least one minute with each book to determine which pile it belongs in. Have them:

   a. read the title

   b. look at the pictures on the front cover

   c. read the back cover (or you read it to them)

   d. flip through a few pages to see if the pictures, font, and layout appeal to them.

4. Make sure your child goes through each of the four steps above with each book—it doesn't need to take more than one minute for each book. These steps teach optisensory learners the nuts and bolts of book selection and how to consistently choose ones they will like. Traditional learners don't need to be taught how to do this—optisensory learners do!

5. After ten minutes your child should have sorted all the books into three piles. If you, their parent, have done the prescreening and selected ten books from within their preferred genre, your child should have put at least three books in the high interest pile.

6. Have your child look at which books they have stacked in the high interest pile. Now it is time for them to arrange them in their final reading order—have them identify which book they will read first, second and third. Have them make three bookmarks and tuck them away in the front of each book so they will remember the chosen reading order.

7. Find a bag around your house or purchase a new one that can serve as your child's presorted book bag. If they can design or embellish a bag it will bring more excitement into the process.

If you have followed all the steps in this book sort method, your child should be feeling a fair amount of anticipation about knowing there are three books waiting for them when reading time arrives. Like previewing movies before going to one, your child has done a book preview and will know what the book is about when reading time comes. How many times have you walked into a movie blindly, or had no idea about a book you were about to start reading? Seldom, if ever. Optisensory learners usually read blindly until they are taught to preview and select books that appeal to their natural interests.

This book sort method can consistently be used at home, in bookstores, and at libraries with children. Over time they will know how to do this on their own in the classroom. Classroom book selection usually goes incredibly wrong for most optisensory learners until they learn how to pick books successfully with this method. Without training your child how to pick books, they will choose books that are either too easy or uninteresting for them. Sometimes they overcompensate and want to appear to friends and teachers that they are more skilled at reading than they actually are. Then they chose books that are objectively beyond their reading ability. When this happens, independent reading in the classroom is a complete waste of time for these children. Productive reading time is what they desperately need.

I always recommend to parents they do book sorts at home and send these high interest books to school with their children so students can make use of the reading time there. I encourage parents to communicate with the classroom teacher about what they are doing and that they would like their support in reminding the student to read the books they have brought from home. I find that teachers are happy to support this approach.

[15]

How A Love of Learning Develops

In my mind, one of the saddest things about teaching missing the mark is the way in which it eclipses the development of a natural love of learning in so many bright children. I believe every person is a natural-born learner. When teaching easily reaches students in the classroom, this natural ability develops into a real and natural love of learning. For traditional learners, this love of learning is ignited by current methods that are designed to reach them.

Being a traditional learner myself, and one who was older than most students, teaching methods reached me, and learning was easy and effortless in my experience. As a result, my natural curiosity was stimulated and fed on a daily basis. I succeeded and was reinforced at school with praise and good grades. This brought about more curiosity and success and became an ever upward-moving spiral of success. I love learning to this day and am still enthralled with expressing my deep curiosity.

But up to 40% of schoolchildren are challenged by traditional teaching, and effortless learning experiences for them rarely occur. Theirs is usually a downward spiral of failure and falling self-esteem.

If you are a traditional learner, it might be hard to imagine what it is like for an optisensory learner in a classroom each day. The best way I can help you to imagine what that is like is to ask you to bring to mind a situation where you remember feeling like a failure, or worse.

I had such an experience recently when I took my new, eight-month-old shelter dog to a dog obedience class. Rohan, a forty-five pound golden retriever mix, has some aggression, and it quickly flared up when we got to the training site. The instructors running the obedience class had no tolerance for his aggression. Right away they put Rohan and I in a corner and actually surrounded us with barricades, explaining it was "good psychologically for the dog." After a while Rohan and I were allowed to return to the group, but I know he and I both were feeling intimidated by our "time-out" in the corner. Now feeling more anxious, in no time at all Rohan pulled his leash free from me and ran over to another dog and became aggressive again. Once again we were sent to the corner and were barricaded for our own good. We eventually finished the class but I was on the verge of tears during the remainder of the session, and I never returned for the other five classes.

The parallel with my dog training story and how optisensory students feel is that each and every day these students feel like I did in the dog training class: intimidated, confused, angry, and upset. The difference, of course, was that I could choose to stop attending the obedience class. A nontraditional student cannot choose to stop attending school, although they often wish they could.

I cannot imagine having to return to a classroom and experiencing such strong feelings of incompetency and failure every day.

I hope you see by now what shaky ground these optisensory learners are on, and how, given the mismatched teaching methods that are coming at them, it's a challenge for them to develop any real love of learning. Resistance, hopelessness and anxiety are the hallmarks of their experience, not hope, enthusiasm, and boundless curiosity.

When a child's school experience fails to cultivate curiosity and self-satisfaction in their hearts and minds, they become adults who lack easy access to some of the emotional states which are key to leading a happy life.

MISPLACED GUILT

When I meet people in public, it is not uncommon for me to talk about what I do with OptiKodes. It happens at coffee shops, restaurants, book stores, or sometimes when I am out at a dog park with Rohan. It never takes long for the person I have just met to respond quite emotionally when I explain about the hidden teaching epidemic and how it derails so many children's success and creates anxiety and self-doubt for them. Literally every new person I explain this to in public tells me about someone they know who they believe has been a casualty in this hidden epidemic. Fathers, siblings, spouses, friends, neighbors, coworkers—everyone knows someone they can identify as having been negatively affected by struggles at school, some of them profoundly.

Earlier this year I was in a coffee shop sharing a table with an older man. He was curious when he saw the large graphic of OptiKodes on the top of my screen and asked if I was writing a book. When I said I was, he asked me what OptiKodes were. My explanation was short, but he connected the dots right away. "I think my son was an optisensory learner," he began. "School was always hard and he never did well or liked it." When I asked where his son was now, he told me he was in prison. He went on to say that he wished he had done more to help his son with school, and that if he had been a better father and helped him more with his school work, his son would have gotten a high school diploma and stayed out of jail.

With a great deal of compassion I explained to this gentleman that likely nothing he did or didn't do would have changed his son's situation back then. I talked a bit more about how his son had gotten caught up in the hidden teaching epidemic and that the cards had been stacked against him all the time. Teaching bias, not this father's support, was the underlying problem for his son, I assured him. When he heard this, the man teared up and said how glad he was to finally realize that it wasn't his fault. As he got up to leave, I could see the weight of the world had been lifted from his shoulders. Human beings can deal with the hardest of life circumstances when they can see how the truth of a situation is operating in their lives. Until the conversation with me, this father didn't understand what had gone wrong. He went away freed from a sense of guilt and failure that was never his to feel.

This is an indelible part of the hidden teaching epidemic— misplaced guilt and blame. As was true with the elderly man just mentioned, family members of struggling optisensory learners often feel their child's learning difficulties are their fault. In fact, I got a call earlier today from the stepfather of a twenty-year-old woman who recently failed the state licensing exam for cosmetology school. He had been referred to me by a therapist who knows of my work and sends families to me when there is a struggling learner. This stepfather began talking about his stepdaughter's life in early grade school, describing how she had been put into a special program in third grade for Spanish-speaking students instead of the regular classroom. He was sure that experience had derailed his stepdaughter, and he was still feeling guilty about it because, as he said, "he could have or should have prevented that third-grade classroom placement."

Here again, I assured this man that his stepdaughter's third-grade placement was not a key factor in her current difficulty. I explained that she is probably a nontraditional learner who had been unintentionally handicapped each year of her education. Now she was still paying a high price. I will send her the OptiKode Assessment and review her results. I would almost bet my life on the fact that her reading is dormant in her OptiKode, and that this is the factor which has put her at risk to underperform throughout school, and is now keeping her from passing an all-important licensing exam she needs to start her career. The caller today was relieved to hear me say that it was misteaching, not his actions or inaction over ten years ago, which had held up his daughter's reading and test-taking skills.

[16]

Limitless Minds

I trust by now that you see how OptiKodes help reveal what our natural-born talents and gifts are and how vital it is that parents protect their children's potential at home with the program. I use the word "potential" here, because in my mind, it is our unique talents and gifts that we develop with our OptiKode that makes up our potential.

As I see it, potential is not some amorphous, "somewhere-in-the-future" ability that will become known to a person when he or she gets there. Instead, in my mind, potential is the fruition of the seeds of ability residing in a person's dominant intelligences that start sprouting early in life just as soon as we start walking, talking, and operating in the world as children.

If circumstances go right for us beginning in the early years and then continue, these seeds of potential gain strength and velocity and sprout into a dazzling full bloom. Once that happens, our potential is ablaze and expresses itself in our life work, our grand passions, and our intimate relationships, which will be explored later in this chapter. External circumstances such as family support, cultural values, health, wealth, and of course our capacity for hard work all contribute to the seeds of potential bearing magnificent fruit in our lives.

The pressure of possible failure and being forced to act and think unnaturally have a significant negative influence on learning effectiveness. Happy relaxed people learn more readily than unhappy stressful people. A person's strength is also a learning channel. A person's weakness is not a great learning channel. Simple, huh?

What if I told you that you could enhance the personal potential of your OptiKode even more? Would it surprise you to hear that it is possible to be highly dominant in all five core intelligences in your OptiKode? What if the limits and boundaries of your OptiKode could be extended, and with it your potential could be expanded too? Would you be interested in upgrading your OptiKode in this way?

I am going to set the stage for talking about how it is possible for any adult to expand the limits of their OptiKode potential by talking about the movie *Limitless* starring Bradley Cooper. If you haven't seen this film, here is a brief recap: early on in the story, Cooper's character, bottoming out in his life, gets hooked on a drug which gives him astounding mental abilities when he is on it. First, he uses his drug-induced mental state to finish writing a book that he has stalled out on completing. He then uses his newfound genius to study the stock market and makes a series of brilliant trades that land him a fortune and ultimately a key position as a partner in one of the best firms on Wall Street.

🎬 Limitless (film) ➜ optiko.de/37

Before long, though, he has to face up to the impossibility of keeping up the charade—the stash of pills which sustains his brilliance are about to run out, and he wonders what will keep his mental abilities and high-end life going. At the end of the film we are amazed to discover that Cooper has been operating without the drugs and that he is still able to sustain his high level of genius and success without them. Somehow his brain has retained its limitless ability, and he is able to stay on top of his game without the drugs.

I was thrilled to see this outcome, not for the generic Hollywood ending that it gives, but because I saw something else being hinted at in the film: that our brains are limitless, and that in a very real way, it is really our beliefs that keep us from seeing how far we can go with our abilities and potential. At some point Cooper realizes this and understands that he has had a limitless potential all along. At the end of the story we see a well-integrated and satisfied Cooper who no longer needs to chase after a drug-induced potential—his real potential has been uncovered and he is finally at peace and united with his limitless mind.

A modern day parable to this film is going on in schools everywhere. We are failing to help children tap into their natural brilliance at school. The result is a tragic loss of limitless potential in all of them, not just the optisensory ones I routinely see who are blowing out of kindergarten in increasing numbers. In the process of teaching in standardized, predictable ways, we are robbing children of a very important piece of self-understanding: how to personally access the limitless abilities which their OptiKodes offer them. Tragically, we are not cultivating a generation of schoolchildren who know how to access the innate strengths of their unique operating system. As a result, we seldom see young adults becoming limitless and breaking the known boundaries of their learning to reach dazzling heights in their lives.

What would the world look like if more people felt in possession of a limitless mind like Cooper's character did? Is there a way that the OptiKodes System might help each individual acquire limitless mental functioning? There absolutely is, and it lies in showing people how to literally "dial up" or amplify the dormant intelligences in their OptiKode. This becomes the next big opportunity with the OptiKodes System: showing virtually every person how to intentionally work at strengthening their dormant OptiKode capacities.

Most of us have heard statements that human beings only use about 20% of their brain power. More is now known about this underutilization phenomenon. Research is revealing that the real state of affairs is that our brains are actually operating at 100% capacity all the time, but that we are just not tapping into it. Something is interfering with our being able to take advantage of this amazing mechanism we call the mind. Connecting the dots isn't hard: we simply have yet to approach learning with young people—or adults—in a manner that would take us beyond the known limits of our minds. I do not want to lay all responsibility on schools and the education system here. Learning is a lifelong phenomenon, and school is just one forum preparing the old and the young to learn. In other words, I for one do not expect schools to do it all.

What if we got to the point of realizing that there could be other mechanisms in society for the lifelong training of our minds? I actually think that we are at this point, and that is why I have designed OptiKodes to be used at home by parents and by adults at any age and from any walk of life. With the Internet fueling our interconnectivity, I think we will be seeing more and more programs such as OptiKodes come forward to take our collective learning abilities beyond known limits in the coming decades. Ultimately, such pioneering companies will help to take the entire burden from the K–12 schooling system and shift it to many organizations that will be helping society as a whole develop our minds in new ways and over our entire lifespans.

Part of the breakthrough that the OptiKodes System offers in this regard is to show people how to tap into their underutilized, dormant modalities in their OptiKode. These dormant capacities in our functioning remain relatively untapped, just waiting for ignition in each one of us. Even though these modalities are dormant, they need not remain so. Tapping into them aligns us more fully with the 100% capacity that is already firing in our brains' neurochemistry every instant of our lives. Once we have aligned with our dominant modalities and then add in the strengthening of our dormant intelligences, we take advantage of the underlying brainpower that we already have. When this happens, conditions are optimal for breakthroughs of all kinds, even ones like Cooper's movie depicts.

As you will remember from chapter three, which gives a technical overview of the OptiKodes System, our dormant intelligences are fairly well behind the scenes of our functioning. They are not center stage like our dominant modalities. This means that a person has to bring more conscious effort to amplifying what is most dormant for them in their OptiKode.

The old adage "use it or lose it" applies here. For most everyone, we tend to overlook and underutilize whatever our dormant modalities are. If we are dormant in moving intelligence, for example, we don't go to the gym on a regular basis or take on home improvement projects. The reason for this is that being moving-dormant can result in being less physically coordinated and facile with moving intelligence. With this dormant placement most people tend to be more sedentary. Because you don't consistently use your dormant moving intelligence, it stays dormant—you don't use it, and so you lose it more and more.

Yet should you simply stay resigned to being moving-dormant and accept underdevelopment in this area of your life? In other words, should you accept those limitations as inalterable? Without a baseline understanding of one's predisposition—one's OptiKode— most people may not be able to initiate lasting change. Your Opti-Kodes brings in a level of self-awareness that enables you to be more skillful with yourself and the changes you want to bring about in life. The point here is that any of us can greatly enhance any of our dormant aptitudes and sculpt a better life with conscious effort.

The students who come to me always develop a more limitless dominance of all five of their aptitudes by the time they finish their program with me. It is a thing of awe to see a child who has become functionally dominant across the board. They possess a sense of confidence and ease that sets them apart from their peers. It is an amazing transformation to witness. Originally, they are lacking in motivation and joy when they first arrive, and when they leave, it is clear they feel on top of the world and in possession of full-blown capacity—this feels like a limitless potential. Ironically, they become more well-rounded than their peers who have not had learning difficulties or needed help.

This development of more robust capability, more limitless potential, is available to any adult with the OptiKodes System. When adults take the OptiKode assessment from the website, they not only get their full OptiKode explained, but they also get a list of personal resources and recommendations that are specifically tailored to help them develop their dormant modalities more fully. It is never too late for anyone to begin work on enhancing their OptiKode. The brain is capable of growth and development at any age. Research is showing that seniors who actively work on staying mentally stimulated are less at risk for age-related issues such as memory loss, dementia and depression.

In my own case, had I known my OptiKode when I began college, not only would I have not pursued training to become a clinical psychotherapist, but I would also have begun enhancing my hearing modality as I bridged into adulthood. For the last several years I have been consciously working to improve my hearing aptitude, and I am seeing improvement. Some of the things I do include taking singing lessons and working on creating characters' voices when I read books. I also create actual voices for friends or colleagues when I read their emails and texts. I was unable to "hear" these voices in the past, but now I hear them on a routine basis. It deepens my engagement with reading books, email, and text correspondence, and literally accesses more of my brain in the process.

In addition, my public speaking abilities are improving by recording my voice and listening to it when I prepare for workshops. I also use voice activation on my iPhone when I do all my text messaging. This may sound simple, but it is a very powerful technique to get better at enunciation and improving my verbal communications skills. I imagine I probably spend ten minutes total each day doing this kind of voice work, just sending voice activated texts alone. This is an hour of explicit audio enhancement work each week, four hours a month, and twelve hours in each quarter of a year; a lot of practice is happening for me with this one technique alone. Can you see how explicit focus on one of your modalities with several separate training techniques could really make a difference in your functioning of that one modality alone? People who do this kind of training, myself included, report feeling more capable in that realm of functioning through the practice they give themselves. This leads to more enhanced well-being and to feeling that one is reaping the benefits of lifelong learning as an adult.

Harkening back to the movie *Limitless*, it really is possible to go beyond our known limits with the OptiKodes System and experience increased potential and life satisfaction through the resources it offers. I can't promise that you will rise to the heights Bradley Cooper's character does, but I can promise that you will feel a growing sense of competency and greater potential in areas of your life that you have felt less confident in. Increased productivity, better work relationships, new hobbies, and more mental energy result when adults push beyond their known limits and use OptiKodes in conscious ways.

[17]

OptiKodes in the Workplace

With OptiKodes, standardization comes to an end. I want to reiterate that the process of standardization that children must somehow manage to endure goes out with them into the world, into every nook and cranny of their lives, whether or not they thrived in school. As adults, we live the values that we are taught in our childhoods. The value of standardization is at the top of the list in the lives of any child who attends a school that is organized in a standardized way—most schools. A few students are lucky enough to attend schools which are not standardized; the Waldorf School and Sudbury Schools are two examples of schools which are about as opposite from standardization as they come.

I venture to guess that at least 90% of children attend a standardized school of some form. You might be surprised to hear that most private schools as well as Christian schools are also standardized, but I can assure you they are. The outcome of all of this is that children spend their lives from ages five to eighteen in a standardized environment, and then go on to find themselves in standardized workplaces, volunteer organizations, and even families of their own creation.

What do I mean when I say a family, a work setting, or a volunteer agency is standardized? To answer that, I want to revisit what I wrote about earlier in the book as I discussed the social forces in the early 1900s which greatly influenced how public education was designed. You may remember that discussion of how as a society we were aligning with the process of mass production, and how factory work and industrialization put a premium on "sameness." All cars coming off an assembly line had to be completely identical. Cans filled with beans and other processed foods had to be identical in the same way. Factory workers sat at machines in symmetrical rows and followed the same instructions to make garments which looked exactly alike. This was the essence of standardization: using a uniform method of production that would ensure the same outcome for every item being manufactured. The school system was set up back then along the same lines—every child was expected to learn the same material at the same pace and sit in the same desks using identical books. As I've described in this book, not much has changed from that standardized approach to learning in our present times.

Looking beyond the classroom, though, I find that most every sphere of life is also standardized. In the work world, one basic organizational approach is held constant in most workplaces. Think about your current work environment—isn't there a basic unifying formula that governs all aspects of your work experience? Isn't everyone expected to arrive at the same time, work the same length of time, sit at desks, and take preset breaks and lunch hours? Regularity and uniformity are a constant. Desks are designed to create work stations where employees stay situated in one place and talking is kept to a minimum. Breaks, lunch hours, meetings—it is all prescribed and systemized in most working environments. All of this is truly thought to be optimal for bringing about the greatest productivity and profits in the workplace.

But what if I told you that a more productive work model would be an OptiKode-centric one, where there would be all sorts of options for employees to work according to the true rhythms and needs of their OptiKodes? This might look like offering employees a sliding work time table which enabled them to come later and leave later each day, or work four days a week for ten hours instead of eight hours a day for five? Instead of one desk or office that was assigned them, there would be workstations all around the office that they could rotate among to vary their physical location from time to time. There would be several different stations that facilitated standing while working, stability balls that could be used in various ways in other areas, as well as ways to literally walk around the office to facilitate thinking, collaboration and relaxation. Music would be piped in or encouraged with the use of head phones, and a few large mounted screens that had streaming visuals for visual stimulation would be mounted around the work environment. Employees would be encouraged to use forty-five minute signal alarms that would prompt them to move to another location—implementing "work intervals"—or at least get up out of their chairs for five minutes and get their circulation going if they didn't want to change locations.

These are just a few of many more options that would effectively move any given workplace away from being standardized. Do you think such a work environment would change productivity and bring about greater creativity and productivity in workplaces? I have no question it would—along with mentally and physically exciting employees and tapping into their fuller resources and capacities, I think such a workplace would reduce the kinds of occupational hazards we see increasing in frequency: carpal tunnel syndrome, eye strain, and tension headaches, as well as neck, back, and shoulder pain, that all result from employees spending too many hours staring into screens in fixed positions.

Consider for a moment the state of the art ergonomic upgrades that are being developed and integrated into workstation designs. Although an improvement, the upgrades still reinforce the standardized paradigm of having people sitting in one place and spending the better part of their work day seated and working on computers. Your keyboard, monitor, and desk may be more in harmony with your eye-hand coordination, but you are still being fundamentally tethered to your desk and screen rather than being given a radically different work environment that would signal an end to the standardized paradigm now in place.

I hope too that you see the origins of this workplace standardization, in how we set up standardized classrooms for school age children, and what it is we train them to do from a very early age: to tolerate a daily desk-bound learning environment in the classroom. Is it any surprise that many of these school-age children become adults who continue spending the better part of their days confined to a seat to do their life work? Life work does not have to be spent this way. It can become nonstandardized if we are able to first see how standardized it actually is, and then begin considering the options for liberating the workplace and allowing it to become more dynamic, active and fulfilling.

I want to add to this discussion that one of my strong hopes is that OptiKodes will become a large enough company to need to hire employees and develop into a full-fledged company. Until now, I have worked independently as a learning specialist, and of course my time spent with children is anything but standardized. I hope to have the opportunity to develop the kind of liberated and liberating work environment that I just described. With any luck at all, OptiKodes will become large enough to not only be helping every optisensory child and family in this country, but to also become a model for corporate America and workplaces everywhere, and show how much more creativity and productivity is possible by moving away from standardized work methods.

[18]

OptiKodes for the Helping Professions

As word has gotten out locally about the work I do with OptiKodes, other professionals have shown interest in the program. My primary focus will be to continue empowering parents to use the program at home, as that is where I believe optisensory learners can be helped most. At the same time, I do not want to overlook how powerful this system can be in the hands of therapists, neuropsychologists, developmental pediatricians, social workers, occupational therapists, and resource specialists. Let me describe the interface of these professions and the OptiKodes System, the future I hope to see.

THERAPISTS

There are a number of therapists locally in the Bay Area of Northern California who know about the OptiKodes System and use it to identify optisensory children they work with directly, or who are children in families of people they help. As these therapists have come to know, children who struggle with learning often exhibit marked symptoms of anxiety, depression, and low self-esteem. I know that nowhere in my training to become a psychotherapist did I learn that something as seemingly innocuous as learning struggles could produce such serious mental health symptoms in children as early as kindergarten. If a therapist has not been trained to correlate these symptoms to the underlying cause of learning difficulties, he or she will undoubtedly miss the chance to address their root causes and help parents manage them effectively.

As I have said, one of the most surprising things I encounter with each child who comes to me for help is the depth and severity of their psychological issues. The turnaround is equally amazing. Between the third and the fifth session, a child begins to noticeably calm down and feel motivated and more confident about school and learning. Over the course of the following several months, these children's coping mechanisms continue to improve, and their personality goes through a radical transformation.

However, if a therapist does not have the ability to assess and diagnose whether a child is an optisensory learner, what will they do with the symptoms that a child presents them with? If the child's family is high-functioning in every other way, they may have no other choice but to conclude that the child has an organic anxiety disorder, and recommend that a prescribing doctor be visited to consider a trial of anti-anxiety medication if the symptoms are bad enough, namely worsening panic attacks or obsessive-compulsive behaviors. Or a therapist might refer the anxious or depressed child to a therapy group for teens experiencing anxiety or depression. Here again, though, if a child's problems stems from school difficulty, and they are put in a therapy group with low-functioning students, and the underlying learning problem is still not understood, the group will not be effective, and even worse, may cause them to feel more insecure. Once again, they are put in an intervention program, not unlike what happens for them at school, yet the real problem goes unaddressed. The upshot of all of this is that typically children feel worse about themselves. The therapy group that was supposed to help ends up demoralizing them further—or even worse, strengthens their identification that something is wrong with them.

I hope you can see the value of therapists becoming acquainted with the OptiKodes System. I hope to take this understanding to graduate school programs where master's level students are becoming therapists. Another clear point of delivery in my mind is in colleges where future teachers are working on their credentials. How can we expect teachers to know how to reach optisensory learners when we do not prepare them to do so?

Getting back to empowering therapists in their practices with OptiKodes, there is yet another angle to how OptiKodes can be beneficial to a therapist's practice. It has more to do with the therapist's own OptiKode. Is the therapist aware of their dominant and dormant modalities and any bias resulting from them?

For example, there might have been a way for me to stay practicing as a therapist if I could have worked with my OptiKode more creatively. Sitting in chairs for long stretches of time is quite hard for me given my OptiKode. As I described earlier, I wrote this book in under eight weeks. Even though this was a rather intense approach to writing, it worked better for me to limit the sitting it takes to write a book to eight weeks rather than spread it out over a six month period of time or longer. How could my limitations of sitting have been brought to bear on my role as a therapist? Here are some ideas that might sound avant-garde at first, but which could have worked:

- With certain clients with an OptiKode similar to mine, we could have started the session standing.
- Midway through a client hour I could have initiated a "standing/stretching break."
- I could have had several different chairs to rotate among, including stability balls like the ones I use as chairs with my stu-

dents. My moving-dominant clients would be offered those options as well.

- Some clients might have been open to the idea of "walking therapy." Who says that therapy must be confined to an office and cannot use the outdoors as an occasional office?

These are just a few ideas that could have easily come into play in my role as a therapist if I had elected to stay in the field and practice. No doubt these changes would have made me feel more at home in my true OptiKode and able to continue the work of helping others that I was deeply drawn to do. The point here is that like school, just about everything we do in our lives is standardized. Who says that the practice of psychotherapy or any other profession all has to look the same? We don't realize how standardized all areas of our lives truly are.

Indeed, this "one size fits all" style of life goes beyond the walls of classrooms and flows out into all areas of life: work, home, leisure, etc. Perhaps this is why so many people feel their lives are in a rut. The bias in therapy is: we sit in chairs and don't get up until the hour is over; we talk as the primary modality during the session; and we stay in one location within a building in the same room each meeting.

Likely your eyebrows went up as you read my short list of how I could have made the therapy hour more conducive for me as well as perhaps for my clients. The list of available options is much longer, inexhaustible in some ways. The fact that you probably saw my short list as somewhat radical speaks to the underlying standardization that exists as the norm in therapy. You would not be alone; standardization is everywhere we look, and it simply begets standardization from us whether we know it or not. There is a flip side to the standardization coin I just presented as it applies to therapists. That flip side has to do with the client. Not only can OptiKodes help therapists be more in sync with their clients as they practice, but they can be used to help clients be more at home in theirs as well. If a therapist knew his or her clients' OptiKodes, they would have more tools to be more intentional and effective with them.

Most of us think that the de facto, most important element in the conventional therapy hour is talking. Do you see how we place the hearing intelligence at the top of the priority list in this regard? But what if the client in front of you is hearing-dormant like I am? Would talking be the best way to help me or another hearing-dormant client resolve their deepest, most intractable complexes and neuroses in therapy? Would it not be compelling to try and meet the client on the home field of their OptiKode and effect change in a way that reaches them more intimately and personally? As I have stated in this book, each and every one of us can be engaged more deeply and meaning-fully when learning methods are synced to our OptiKode. This holds true in therapy—we can sync therapy to our clients by knowing their OptiKodes.

What would syncing therapy with clients' OptiKodes look like? Here is a short list of things that could be implemented with a client who is seeing-dominant:

- Direct them to look at evocative art to stimulate a deeper connection to their inner resources.
- Have them bring in photos of loved ones, living or deceased, or their childhood homes, and have them access these photos throughout the therapy hour.
- Ask them to visually focus on objects in the room to bring about more embodied presence.
- Make paper, pens, and other multimedia available for clients so they can draw their experience rather than exclusively verbalize it.

Can you see in all of these ideas that the shift would be away from a full reliance on talking as the preferred and superior mode of doing therapy? I have heard from therapists who have tried some of these techniques that they have opened up sessions in new and effective ways. Working in a multimodal way that is truly "client-centric" can be more engaging and liberating than remaining standardized in one's approach. It can create a win-win situation that brings more aliveness and dynamism into human interactions of all kinds.

DEVELOPMENTAL PEDIATRICIANS

In the same way that OptiKodes can help both therapists and therapy clients receive more benefit in their work together, I believe developmental pediatricians as a group can be an important resource in bringing the value of the OptiKodes System forward to families who desperately need the benefit of its understanding. You might argue that pediatricians should only be involved when it comes to affecting the health and wellness of their patients and should stay at arm's length when it comes to the arena of the mind and learning with families and children in their medical practices. I believe very differently—it is because learning difficulties produce many physical symptoms and mental health issues in children that doctors should in fact know how to utilize the OptiKodes System in their medical practices and assess children's symptoms as possibly being related to children being left behind and struggling in school.

As I just talked about with the OptiKodes assessment and its use in therapy, what does a doctor do with the symptoms of anxiety, depression, or sleeplessness they might see in a young child? What comes up as underlying causes in a pediatrician's mind when they see such symptoms in their young patients? If a doctor does not connect such symptoms to the struggles at school that may be generating them, what then are they going to diagnose and treat? A doctor in this situation will likely order tests for other disorders that can cause deeper depression or anxiety. If they are ruled out, what then? Not finding a clear cause, a pediatrician may find themselves prescribing an antidepressant or anxiety medication. While some relief may occur doing this, the underlying cause goes undiagnosed, and a medicated student's symptoms will not be resolved no matter what combination of medication the doctor prescribes. Many people would also agree that we are overmedicating the population. Do we really support the use of medication for a struggling schoolchild when the real cure can be as simple a syncing the teaching to the student?

How incredible would it be to have parents take a simple ten-minute assessment given by their child's doctor, which would give them information about whether or not their child was at risk to fall behind and struggle in school, and which further described the options available to prevent that?

I wish this kind of early intervention program would be in place at kindergarten registrations every fall, but as I think you see by now, the traditional school system is blind to its bias and its hidden effects. Developmental pediatricians are not part of that system, and as such, have a pivotal role to play in stopping this epidemic from continuing to afflict children everywhere. Education is a mighty force, and I am hoping that pediatricians will be called to take up a new and vital role in the education of families about the effects of learning difficulties and how to address them in an effective way. Their inclination to do so would be in alignment with their focus on childhood development. Few things are as impactful on a child's development as being unintentionally handicapped by traditional teaching methods that derail their normal development and which can, and often do, generate acute physical and mental health symptoms in many children.

SOCIAL WORKERS, OCCUPATIONAL THERAPISTS, AND RESOURCE SPECIALISTS

Returning to the discussion of how OptiKodes can bring more vitality and success to the helping professions, I want to touch on a few more obvious ones. I see that social workers, OTs, and Resource Specialists are good candidates for integrating the OptiKodes System into their practices. Since these professionals often work with children and families who struggle, the knowledge that OptiKodes offer can make their interventions more powerful and long-lasting. I know that social work, for example, often involves direct intervention with the whole family in their homes instead of in an office. Being able to do an additional family-wide assessment that OptiKodes makes possible would give a social worker a wealth of information not only about which children are at risk in school, but what the entire family dynamic looks like given the constellation of OptiKodes in the family.

An occupational therapist, on the other hand, would get the benefit of learning what a child's dominant learning modalities are, and would thus be able to closely integrate that knowledge into their overall treatment plan. Someone who primarily practices neurosensory integration work with children and adolescents would be wise to know what their clients' OptiKodes are to get the additional benefit of syncing learning interventions to their OptiKode.

A good example to illustrate how this would work is as follows: I had a boy who was diagnosed with both Asperger's and an auditory processing disorder. Given his diagnosis, his mother and the OT working with him were both of the mind that he was not a learner who would benefit by audio interventions. My OptiKode assessment revealed however, that he was Hearing #1 in his OptiKode, so I knew that despite his auditory processing deficit, he actually did learn best by hearing. I used very explicit audio tools and strategies with him, and he made very rapid progress, which surprised both his mother and the OT. I was not surprised, however. As I mentioned in chapter twelve in the discussion of learning disabilities, ADD, and ADHD, children with disabilities need the benefit of the OptiKodes System as much as, if not more, than nontraditional, optisensory learners.

Based on my experience with struggling learners, I know this: they must be given a radically different program than the traditional one that has not reached them in the classroom. How wonderful it would be to imagine a pirate—or space exploration—intervention room in school where struggling learners could have an effective and fun-filled interventions program made available to them in school. I would prefer, of course, that the classroom itself changed, so that teaching became child-centric in the first place. But failing that, if pull-out programs were at least multimodal and resource specialists could identify the OptiKode of the child in front of them, and thereby know how to most effectively reach them, learners would quickly get to grade level and no longer be behind and stay behind. The stigma would be a lot less debilitating as a result. Every child in the class would wish for regular visits to the pull-out room at school.

As for resource specialists who work privately, learning the Opti-Kodes System would enable them to do more targeted and rapid work with their students, and they would be able to dial parents in as well to keep the benefits of optisensory learning on board at home as well. As I've shared earlier, I think it is truly the ethical thing to do to educate parents so they know as much about the system as the specialist does. The need for optisensory learning remains constant for these learners every day of their lives. I believe home has got to be the place where parents have the know-how and tools to keep the system alive and well for their children throughout the rest of their school years.

[19]

Career Planning with OptiKodes

Are you someone, like myself, who has changed careers at some point in your working life? Or are you perhaps on the verge of a major change in your current job or profession? If so, the reason you made the change you did may have been to get into closer alignment with your unique OptiKode. Let me explain a little more using my own experience as an example.

I obtained a pre-law undergraduate degree—thinking that I was headed to law school—then went to graduate school to become a clinical psychotherapist instead. Being a therapist seemed like the right calling for me. I was drawn to helping people and got feedback that I was empathic and highly intuitive with people—some of the qualities good therapists must have. After getting my degree and working a number of years, I took a sabbatical from being a therapist to help my daughter through the lengthy illness I described earlier in the book. Oddly, I never went back when she recovered. I simply wasn't drawn back to working as a therapist and got drawn instead into working as a trainer and curriculum designer for the pioneering education company I mentioned. For years I wondered if I would return to being a therapist and for the most part thought that I had just "put the pause button on." Years later, when I had developed the OptiKodes System to a certain point, I finally connected the dots: my work as a therapist was simply not in alignment with my OptiKode.

In my own OptiKode my moving intelligence is #1, and thus most dominant (along with seeing). My hearing intelligence—which you need to talk with clients all day—is most dormant. My OptiKode fits a person who has a hard time sitting for very long and talking at length—it is not a good fit for a therapist, I'd say. Had I known this, of course, I would never have chosen a career in therapy. I would have chosen instead the kind of work I do now: working as an educator in a mode which is highly active and hands-on, and which does not require as much talking as classroom teaching does.

At the same time, I must acknowledge that all the international travel and living abroad I did, as well as my degrees in pre-law and psychotherapy, have all contributed a great deal to the work I am doing with OptiKodes. In particular, the part of me that wanted to be a lawyer and fight for justice is doing that right now. I feel that the plight of nontraditional learners is highly unjust, and I am fighting passionately for equality of education for all students every day of my working life. The part of me that wanted to become a therapist and prevent the trauma and suffering of children is certainly doing that now with OptiKodes.

While I don't regret the path I've taken, the fact is that I would never have taken the particular path I did if I had a full, conscious understanding of my OptiKode. I believe this is true for countless other people. If you are someone who made a career change in the past, did you get it right? Do you feel in sync with how you are wired to navigate now? If you haven't already done so, getting your Opti-Kode from the website will help give you the insight to evaluate whether you did get it right and are in a profession or job that is more synchronized with your operating system. If you aren't feeing at home or happy in your current job or profession, chances are you are still out of sync with your OptiKode.

Likewise, if you are on the verge of making a change, you would be wise to consult your OptiKode and make sure you are headed in the right direction. We choose jobs and professions for all sorts of reasons: their starting salary or wage; their status; the family mold—being a doctor like dad or a teacher like mom; "the path of least resistance;" or "I'm too old to go back to school now." There are other reasons you might have come up with to choose the job you did, but the fact of the matter is that unless your career choice is in sync with your innate abilities, your daily work life may be unsatisfactory. An important ingredient for happiness will still be missing from your life.

Books such as *What Color Is Your Parachute* and *Do What You Love and the Money Will Follow*, while helpful, still lack the laser-like focus of how and why you will thrive in a particular job or industry that an OptiKode can give you. Yes, it is true that you must love what you do when you head in a particular job direction, but love may not be enough. Indeed, if you only consider love, you might find yourself in a career that is still a mismatch with your OptiKode. Take me—I really did love being a therapist, but that career is not the one that I could sustain for a lifetime given my particular OptiKode. I was lucky to finally arrive at the right career for my OptiKode. Some people don't get it right even the second or third time around. I think at that point, many people just give up and resign themselves to a lower level of life satisfaction.

As for those of us who make just one major career change and get it right, we often fall into the category of being "late bloomers." That is certainly true for me; I feel like am just hitting my stride with the OptiKodes System after changing careers fourteen years ago.

Another thing worth mentioning here is that when a person's career is nicely synced up with their OptiKode, they stand a much higher chance of becoming a specialist or "subject matter expert" in the line of work they do. I talked earlier about how each OptiKode is a key to a particular specialization in the world and how important it is for schools to become deeply interested in unlocking the key of every learner's individual genius. I believe that few people can go on to become subject matter experts if they are out of sync with their OptiKode in the work they do. This is because when we are working in accordance with our OptiKode, we generally love what we do, and it often doesn't feel like "work" at all to us. Instead, we feel deeply compelled and fascinated by the work we do, and it draws out our inherent abilities and gifts as much as our passion. That kind of experience is utter satisfaction.

On this point about passion, I can share with you that the writing of this book has been one of the most consummately enjoyable experiences of my life. There was literally not a single moment of writer's block or frustration that occurred during the writing of it—it was truly a "labor of love" from the first moment on. The writing literally flowed out of me in an unstoppable current over the course of just six weeks of writing, in which I spent an average of 4.5 hours a day writing. I never felt tired or drained. I got less sleep than usual, but always awoke filled with energy and excitement to return to the next day's writing.

When I recently saw the movie *Jobs*, I realized that in Steve Jobs I was seeing a clear and shining example of someone who followed the calling of his OptiKode and lived in utter faithfulness to it. As far as I could tell, his burning passion and genius resulted from him aligning with his OptiKode and unleashing his unparalleled vision for personal computing onto the world as a result. This kind of passion and creativity is possible for each one of us when we liberate the treasures of our mind and functioning by finally getting our OptiKode right and finding the most fulfilling jobs and professions for ourselves.

OptiKodes in the Writing Professions

I don't think it will surprise you when I say that I have developed a way to help writers take advantage of the OptiKodes System. I have loved writing my entire life, and the whole topic is very near and dear to me. As I wrote in chapter thirteen, handwritten language is imperiled, and I hope to be a voice in an important dialogue about preventing its extinction. When it comes to the art of writing, it turns out that the OptiKodes System can be of real benefit. I have shared with you how this system can help parents pick the right books for their children, and now I want to describe how this system can be used by people to become better writers.

Think about it for a moment—doesn't it make sense that like everything else we do in our daily lives, when it comes to the act of writing, we would do it according to our OptiKode? Doesn't it make sense that someone with a moving-dominant plus seeing-dominant Opti-Kode would write novels that are packed with action, adventure and a lot of visual imagery? I had a very interesting conversation last weekend with an author who is Thinking #1 and who has written three science fiction novels. To begin with, because he is so logical, writing science fiction novels makes perfect sense. Like others who are thinking-dominant, he has a penchant for imagining futuristic worlds with highly technical features and creating plot lines loaded with invented technologies of all kinds.

As we talked and I asked him more questions about his most recent book, I could tell that he was likely seeing-dormant in his Opti-Kode. His novel sounded short on visual descriptions; the technical side of things was amplified. However, unlike the movie *Avatar*, he had created a world more technical, or logical in nature, but not as filled with visual imagery. As a writer he would appeal to readers like himself who are also thinking-dominant and seeing-dormant. Someone like me who is very seeing-dominant would be left feeling somewhat dissatisfied. This kind of thing is typical with most writers. The dormant intelligences in their OptiKode become the weak elements in their writing. OptiKodes can shine a light on your natural strengths and weaknesses and help you become more skillful in reaching any person's OptiKode with your writing.

Another example is a project of mine—the backstory of *Seamour's Reading*, a reading program I developed for parents and children to use at home, which will be available on the OptiKodes website. Seamour is a ten-legged "dectopus"—he has two more tentacles than the average octopus. Along with several memorable sea creatures and two optisensory children named Dalton and Ali, Seamour creates a game with the "10 Terrific Reading Tricks" his great-grandfather Seamus taught him when he was a young dectopus. These tricks make reading successful and a blast for children and their parents to do together at home and quickly accelerate early elementary schoolchildren's reading progress.

The tie-in with *Seamour's Reading* and my own dormant OptiKode skills came to my attention when my daughter edited the backstory of *Seamour's Reading* that comes with the reading kit. After my daughter read it, she told me that although she could really see the setting and characters—seeing-dominant—as well as vividly experience all the excitement throughout the fifteen-page story—moving-dominant—she couldn't "hear the dialogue" very well. "I know what you meant to say, mom, I just couldn't hear the voices," she told me.

Right away I saw my dormant hearing in action. Writing dialogue is my weak spot, since I am hearing-dormant. My daughter's comments confirmed what I already know about my weak spot in writing. She is currently editing the story and dialogue in *Seamour's Reading*, and once she can hear the voices come to life, I am sure the dialogue will hit the sweet spot and finally say things the right way and feel more natural for readers.

It is not as easy as it might sound to be an all-around good writer. Something is usually missing for each one of us. Usually, we just don't know what that something is. Your OptiKode points to the likely weak spots in your writing project and can create breakthroughs for you, so that you can write in a more engaging way. It is a tricky thing to be able to step out of your preset writing disposition and write more comprehensively and in a way which will keep every reader engaged. The OptiKodes System offers you a way to open up your writing process, so you can become the well-received author you want to be.

The same set of OptiKode writing principles that apply to authors of fiction and nonfiction hold true for anyone who creates websites, PowerPoint presentations, and even such things as TED talks. The best projects or videos in all those categories are the ones that are truly multimodal: they leave no single modality out. Part of my expertise is the ability to examine all kinds of presentations and give feedback about how multimodal each one is.

In my experience, only about 25% of most projects and videos I see are multimodal. I always believe that the limitations I see match the dormant modalities of the creator's OptiKode. The best projects I run across are clearly the ones that are close to 100% multimodal. The next time you sit on the edge of your seat with high interest during a presentation or when you are watching a TED talk online, try seeing if you can identify all five modalities in the presentation and feel how this keeps you so engaged. I am including a link here to one that I find very multimodal as an example for you to keep in mind.

🕊 Jake Barton: The museum of you (TED talk) ➜ optiko.de/38

The bottom line is that it is almost impossible to disengage from a presentation if it is engaging all five of your intelligences. When we are engaged with all five modalities, we become completely drawn in and interested—boredom is not a possibility. I can't help but mention that this holds true at school for children too. Unless all five intelligences are used in classrooms, children lose interest and disengage. Even the traditional students are less deeply engaged or interested than they could be. What can look like interest for these strong, thriving traditional students is often compulsive overachievement masquerading as engagement. All children do better when multimodal teaching and learning is underway in the classroom.

OptiKodes for Athletes and Coaches

Another topic which is of huge interest to me is the tie-in between OptiKodes and the sports and athletic world. To begin, let me say how typical and predicable a particular pattern has been to me over the years. The pattern is the extremely athletic and accomplished athlete who struggles with reading and school. One mother, Karen E., who is included in the testimonials at the beginning of the book, has two such children who were behind at school and who learned how to protect their learning and self-esteem with the OptiKodes System. Over the years Karen has referred numerous families to me, all of whom had incredible athletes who were inexplicably struggling at school. Whenever Karen overheard the mother of an athlete talk about their child's school difficulties, she would ask: "Is your child a great athlete but not good at reading? Is he or she an incredible competitor on the field but not able to sit still in the classroom?"

Each of the students and families who Karen referred all fit this profile: they were moving-dominant but reading-dormant in their OptiKode. This is the case for so many athletes in schools everywhere—they are not cut out to learn the old-fashioned, "sit, look, and listen" way and are unintentionally handicapped year-in and year-out. When presented with my BodyPlusLearning program, they and their parents discover how to keep their bodies engaged and central in the learning process.

The hard part about the tragedy for these moving-dominant athletes is how they now fall behind starting early in grade school, and then by high school are teetering on the margin of failing one or more courses all the time. What makes this so tragic is that star athletes whose grades fall below C in their classes can be benched until the next quarter when they get their Ds and Fs back up into the C range or higher.

Isn't this preposterous—we fail to teach in a fair and effective way to these learners, and then take away the one area where they shine as a consequence—their athletics? Is it any wonder why many of them resort to cheating to make the grades both at high school and in college? Probably like me, you have heard stories of athletes who have been caught cheating at college—they have to make the grades in order to compete—and are kicked out of college as a result. Now, I am in no way condoning cheating, but I think it is a travesty of justice to *not* provide them with learning methods that enable them to succeed academically, and then sideline them from competition when their grades suffer, or kick them out of college when they are caught cheating. This is a double bind if ever I heard one.

The last work I did before leaving the field of mental health was to help set up a newly licensed outpatient drug treatment center in Northern California. One part of our center was geared to the "drug court" clients. These were parolees or recently released inmates who had all been incarcerated for drug-related crimes. The idea of drug court was to give them the treatment they needed instead of incarcerating them again. The thing they needed was good treatment, not more jail time. It simply makes good sense, I believe, to treat the problem rather than punish people who have failed because we haven't addressed their underlying problem.

When it comes to cheating in college, my approach would be the same—to assess the student and determine the underlying causes. Is this someone who, by virtue of being a nontraditional learner and a casualty of the hidden teaching epidemic, is now functioning at a low level in college? Wouldn't it make the most sense to give them the same kind of optisensory training my students get, so they finally acquire the skills to get in the game of their academics and stay there?

I live in a neighborhood where there are several nearby communities that are very affluent, and where families of optisensory learners put a high premium on supporting their children's athletics in high school and college. The student whose report I shared earlier to illustrate assessing ADD and ADHD is such a student. He is an exceptional athlete and wants to play sports in college. So much of whether he gets into the college sports program of his choice is riding on him getting the grades those colleges require. He is teetering on the edge of making those grades, so his last senior year's school performance is critical—talk about pressure. The amount of stress he feels around all of this is overwhelming him, and for good reason. I am including this discussion here in the hopes that parents of high school athletes as well as athletic coaches become sensitized to the dilemma which these athletes are in relative to their sports programs and school achievement. Once again, I feel that education and awareness is the critical first step before change can truly happen.

THE COMPETITIVE EDGE

Beyond their ability to help athletes make better grades, OptiKodes can be of benefit for training and competition for athletes and their coaches. To begin with, you can well imagine how many coaches develop a predictable coaching style with the athletes they coach. Their coaching style in most cases is synced to their own OptiKode instead of their athletes. However, with the aid of the OptiKodes System, a coach can come to see what an athlete's dominant modalities are and coach them accordingly, bringing about a higher degree of coaching precision, which in turn brings about better training sessions, skills, and success for the athletes they work with.

As an example, imagine a swimmer who is Moving #1 followed by Hearing #2 and Seeing #3 in their Opti-Kode. Knowing their OptiKode, a coach would tailor his coaching strategies with that swimmer to utilize this athlete's hearing and visual dominance. To sync to this athlete's OptiKode, the coach would primarily focus on verbal input with this swimmer, giving repetitive verbal instructions in such a way that the athlete "really heard" them. In that the athlete is also visually dominant, the coach would then utilize visual strategies. This might look like the coach literally getting in the water and showing the swimmer a certain technique or pointing out another swimmer doing it in the pool. Another visual strategy would be to have the swimmer watch particular videos that demonstrate the skills they need to develop. Lastly, the coach might also film the swimmer and play back the footage to critique their technique.

Other swimmers who are hearing-dormant in their OptiKodes would not benefit as much by a lot of verbal input. In fact, a lot of verbal instruction by the coach could actually interfere with those swimmers improving their technique. With hearing-dormant athletes, a coach would have to work to minimize verbal coaching and would instead sync the coaching to the dominant modalities in those swimmer's OptiKodes. If those swimmers were thinking-dominant and seeing-dominant besides being moving-dominant, it would be best to break coaching down into logical and systematic steps that the swimmers could integrate in a stepwise fashion. Being seeing-dominant as well, these athletes would benefit by the visual strategies described above. Another helpful visual strategy that would be to give the swimmers diagrams

of a stroke being broken down into its component parts that they could study over time. All of these different coaching strategies can be customized for each athlete depending on their OptiKode—the standardization of athletics can be replaced with a more precise and effective approach as a result.

In ending this section on athletes, coaching and the OptiKodes System, I want to say that one of the saddest things about the hidden teaching epidemic for athletes is that they often think they can only shine in the world of competitive sports, and that they seldom develop true confidence in their general learning abilities. What happens when they don't get into the colleges of their choice, get kicked out for cheating, or retire from sports but don't have the confidence to do anything outside of the sporting world? For famous athletes like Tiger Woods or Joe Montana, endorsements and sports announcing produce huge financial rewards during and after their sports careers. For less well-known athletes, however, their options are a lot more limited. That narrowing of options is the invisible endgame that many athletes end up facing, since their full learning potential is seldom supported or reached with standardized education

[20]

Imagine This World

Imagine a world where everyone easily understands that no two brains think alike. In this world there is a system which helps us understand the true uniqueness of our own brain and everyone else's too. Imagine a world where this huge diversity of brain design is tapped into on a daily basis, and where families can fully understand each child and ensure their school success. This is a world where children thrive, where families live in harmony, with mutual understanding and support, and where schools also come on board and make learning a life-changing experience for students every day. This is not a world of the future, it is here now, and can be reached by your stepping across its threshold at our website: OptiKodes.com.

Take the Next Step at OptiKodes Academy

You can quickly see the same kinds of results you read about in the case studies in chapter six by joining the OptiKodes Academy and implementing the OptiKodes System at home. With consistent time and attention, this at-home, parent-led program will produce the same kind of breakthroughs in your family. Your child will show these new behaviors after a fairly short time:

- coming to you interested in doing their homework instead of staging resistance and battles after school
- actually learning their subjects instead of simply memorizing information for a test
- being excited about going to school and learning
- feeling proud about test scores that are now consistently in the proficient range
- becoming a student who wants to take on new challenges and excel even more
- appearing confident and happy in every part of their life.

🌐 Parents Speak about OptiKodes (video) ➜ optiko.de/2v

The Secret Sauce

You can't learn the OptiKodes System by simply reading a book—parents need to see how optisensory learning actually looks in order to learn how to do it themselves. Therefore, Ms. Blackburn has opened up her practice and created an ever-expanding video library for parents. These training videos are from actual lessons with children she currently teaches. They have been filmed and prepared for you to learn from. You can watch them as often as you'd like and can stay abreast of new videos as they are developed. The mission of the

OptiKodes Academy is to make you the expert in your child's success. That is why the OptiKodes Academy is the family-friendly place to learn how to learn.

The main areas of the website include:

- the free Child OptiKode Assessment which confirms whether or not your child is an optisensory learner
- parent testimonials
- introductory videos
- articles on multisensory learning, optisensory learning, education reform, products and learning aids, books, and more
- links to other sites and resources.

Membership in the OptiKodes Academy includes:

- 12 pages of explanation for each family member's OptiKode
- a Learning Shift Guide that begins your training program
- unlimited webinars where you have the opportunity to interact with Ms. Blackburn
- a members' forum where you can interact with other members
- unlimited access to the OptiKodes Academy's video library which cover these topics and more:
  - working with specific elements of the OptiKodes
  - BodyPlusLearning: an essential program for supporting the high energy, kinetic child
  - motivating your child with an action-packed and competitive incentive system
  - explicit tools and techniques for each intelligence modality
  - how to apply these tools and techniques in the proper order for specific OptiKodes
  - a remedial reading program for all grade levels
  - how parents can learn to "shift and sync" to their child's OptiKode
  - how to choose the right books for your child

- how optisensory learners can more effectively study
- fun and effective strategies for spelling tests
- ending homework wars—making homework fun and effective.

Many videos show actual optisensory learners in session with Ms. Blackburn; others are specific videos introducing tools and techniques without students. For parents, the video library is the resource that helps you keep getting better and better at empowering your child. There is no other resource available that is this extensive and offers parents the ongoing support needed to turn their optisensory child's learning around.

Using these videos and then practicing the new techniques with your child, his or her basic foundational skills will develop immediately and set the stage for ongoing learning and success. With parents taking the lead, their son or daughter's breakthroughs will stay with them through high school and beyond, because children will have "learned how to learn," which is a powerful thing to learn at any age.

🌐 OptiKodes Academy ➜ OptiKodes.com

ABOUT THE AUTHOR

Kimberley Blackburn has worked as a Learning Specialist in private practice for over fourteen years. As a former child and adolescent therapist, she saw the emotional consequences of learning difficulties on children's self-esteem and confidence. She became determined to unravel the mystery of why so many bright kids struggle in school. Her work with hundreds of struggling students led to the development of the OptiKodes System, which shows parents how to support their child's unique approach to learning.